down to
earth

down to **earth**

Solid Waste Disposal for Low-Income Countries

Mansoor Ali, Andrew Cotton
and Ken Westlake

Water, Engineering and Development Centre
Loughborough University
1999

Water, Engineering and Development Centre
Loughborough University
Leicestershire
LE11 3TU UK

© WEDC, Loughborough University, 1999
Reprinted in 2019

This publication is also available online at:
https://wedc-knowledge.lboro.ac.uk/details.html?id=16572

Ali, S.M., Cotton, A.P. and Westlake, K. (1999)
Down to Earth: Solid Waste Disposal for Low-Income Countries,
WEDC, Loughborough University, UK.

ISBN 13 Paperback: 9780906055663
ISBN Library Ebook: 9781788532914
Book DOI: http://dx.doi.org/10.33629781788532914

A catalogue record for this book is available from the British Library.

This document is an output from a project funded by the UK
Department for International Development (DFID)
for the benefit of low-income countries.
The views expressed are not necessarily those of DFID.

This edition reprinted and distributed by Practical Action Publishing.
Since 1974, Practical Action Publishing has published and disseminated books and
information in support of international development work throughout the world.
Practical Action Publishing trades only in support of its parent charity objectives
and any profits are covenanted back to Practical Action
(Charity Reg. No. 247257, Group VAT Registration No. 880 9924 76).

Designed and produced at WEDC
Cover photograph: Down to earth: picking metals from ashes
after burning waste at a disposal site in Karachi.

About the Authors

Dr Mansoor Ali is a Project/ Programme Manager at WEDC. A specialist in solid waste management for low-income countries, he has researched and published extensively on the subject and is currently involved with the research projects *Capacity Building, Micro-enterprise Development* and *Appropriate Landfilling.*

Dr Andrew Cotton is the Director of Urban Programmes WEDC. A specialist in urban infrastructure for low-income countries, some of his recent research includes micro-contracts, operation and maintenance, knowledge management and urban sanitation.

Dr Ken Westlake is an associate at Land Quality Management Ltd. He has undertaken a number of research projects in anaerobic bacterial metabolism, including the degradation of wastes in landfills. At AEA Technology he managed an extensive landfill research programme and as a lecturer at Loughborough University taught hazardous waste management. He has a number of years experience in the management of wastes with particular interests in sustainable waste management, including landfill.

Acknowledgements

The following persons made valuable contributions to this research:

Local Collaborators

Rehan Ahmed	Association for Protection of Environment, Karachi
Paul Arnold	Arba Minch Water Technology Institute, Arba Minch
Mansoor Imam	NED University of Engineering and Technology, Karachi
Shahid Mahmood	Community Action Programme, Faisalabad.

Peer Reviewers

David Campbell	AEA Consultants, UK
Adrian Coad	SKAT, Switzerland
Graham Cooper	DFID, UK
Manus Coffey	Manus Coffey and Associates, Ireland
Jane Olley	ERM Consultants, UK
Jeremy Colins	Freelance Consultant

Others

Jenny Appleton	WEDC, UK
Rod Shaw	WEDC, UK

Contents

List of Boxes

List of Tables

List of Figures

List of Photographs

Acronyms

CBO	Community Based Organisation
DFID	Department for International Development
DMO	District Management Offices
IWB	Itinerant Waste Buyer
KDA	Karachi Development Authority
KMC	Karachi Metropolitan Corporation
RDF	Refuse Derived Fuel
SWM	Solid Waste Management
UNEP	United Nations Environment Programme
Rs	Rupees, Pakistani currency (1 US $ = Rs 55 in 1999)

Glossary

Acetogenic
When the organic material in the waste is deprived of oxygen but has sufficient moisture, it undergoes anaerobic decomposition. This decomposition goes through two phases — the first phase is the acetogenic phase in which acids form.

Anthropogenic
Man-made.

Attenuate
The process of weakening, for example, by dilution, adsorption etc. In an unconfined landfill site the leachate is allowed to migrate into the surrounding environment but the risk posed by the leachate is low due to the diluting affects.

BOD/COD/TOC
Biological Oxygen Demand, Chemical Oxygen Demand, Total Organic Carbon. Measurements of the carbonaceous content.

Calorific value
The amount of heat that can be produced from the substance.

Crude tipping
The uncontrolled disposal of solid waste to un-designated areas.

Engineered disposal
In engineered disposal the waste is disposed of in a fully controlled manner with maximum protection to the environment.

Environmental hazard
An event/situation which is potentially harmful to the environment.

Eutrophication/eutrophic state
To make rich in nutrients to such an extent that excessive plant growth kills animal life by the deprivation of oxygen.

Explosive range
The range of concentrations at which a gas (e.g. hydrogen or methane) is explosive.

Fail safe landfill
A landfill in which any releases should pose no unacceptable risk to the environment.

Geomembranes	Synthetic membranes used as landfill liners to contain leachate, typically made from high or medium density polyethylene.
Global warming	The warming of the earth's atmosphere by the accumulation of gases that absorb reflected solar radiation.
Heterogenous	Composed of diverse elements.
Landfill cap	The covering layer of a filled landfill.
Leachate	The polluted water which flows from a landfill.
Lithology	The nature or composition of stones or rocks.
Methanogenic	The second phase of anaerobic decomposition is the methanogenic phase in which methane gas is formed.
Sanitary landfill	The highest standard of disposal-to-land operation. It is a planned facility that is constructed and operated in such a way that environmental pollution and nuisance from the site are kept to a minimum, both during operation and after the site is closed. The waste may be placed below or above the level of the surrounding ground.
Saturated (groundwater) zone	The zone beneath the water table.
Unsaturated (vadose) zone	The unsaturated zone below the earth's surface and above the water table.
Waste composition	An assessment of the different components of the waste. Often expressed as percentage of wet weight of the major components e.g. paper, cardboard, plastics, metals etc.
Water balance [negative/positive]	The net amount of water/free leachate retained at the site (i.e. leachate production minus leachate leaving site.)

Section 1

Introduction and Background

This document presents a framework for selecting feasible options for the disposal of municipal solid waste in low income countries. It is the final output from Project R6842 *Appropriate Landfilling of Solid Waste* carried out by the authors as part of the Technology, Development and Research (TDR) Programme, Engineering Division, Department for International Development (DFID) of the British Government. It has been written for policy makers and professional staff of urban government, development agencies and non-government organisations in low income countries.

The purpose of this output is to help improve the poor practices of municipal solid waste management that prevail in many low income countries — a subject that has received scant attention when compared to other aspects of infrastructure such as water supply and transport. It is a complex topic embracing waste collection, transfer, haulage and disposal and its impacts are wide, including, for example, effects on environmental health, municipal finance and management, waste reuse, and informal sector employment. It is therefore important to take a broad view and not to consider disposal options within the narrow confines of a particular technology. This work is drawn mainly from available literature and gives particular emphasis to the principle of building on existing municipal capacity.

Despite the relatively large body of work on high technology options for waste disposal, there is very little material appropriate for low income countries. It is therefore possible that inappropriate, expensive and unmanageable disposal systems are being implemented in many places — if there is a planned system at all. This work helps to remedy the current deficiency through review, analysis and adaption of existing material and the use of case study material from the cities of Karachi and Faisalabad in Pakistan, and Addis Ababa and Arba Minch in Ethiopia. All were visited as part of this work, with Karachi being presented here as a case study.

A detailed literature review was conducted at the outset of the project. This is a stand-alone document and is available on request. The list of references and a short bibliography for further reading are included in this document.

The document is divided into five sections:

Section 1: Short introduction to the research

Section 2: Description of various options for the disposal of municipal solid waste

Section 3: Framework for the selection of disposal options which considers technical, institutional, financial, social and environmental factors

Section 4: Application of the framework to the case study of Karachi, Pakistan

Section 5: Review of the available guidelines for planning landfill, keeping in view the situation in low-income countries.

Section 2

Options for Municipal Waste Disposal

The context

Safe disposal of municipal solid waste is important for the protection of both public health and the city environment. This protection should be sustainable, dealing with today's waste today without passing on problems to future generations (Westlake, 1995). Unfortunately, indiscriminate dumping around cities in low income countries is very common and creates numerous problems:

Box 1. Hazards of indiscriminate dumping of solid waste

- Health hazards to the nearby residents through inhalation of dust and smoke from burning of waste.

- Environmental pollution from smoke.

- Environmental pollution from waste leachate and gas.

- Blockage of open drains and sewers, creating serious secondary problems relating to public health and environmental pollution.

- Health hazards to waste workers and pickers through direct contact with waste.

Constraints

There are many reasons why safe disposal is rarely practised in low income countries, Box 2 identifies some of the key issues. Improvements to waste disposal practices depend largely on overcoming these constraints, gradually. This document aims to provide broad technical guidance, but detailed solutions to most problems need to be worked out within the local context.

Box 2. Key issues in solid waste disposal

1. Municipal capacity

- The scale of the task can be enormous. The city of Karachi, for example, generates more than 6000 tonnes of domestic solid waste daily of which the Metropolitan Corporation manages to collect only 60%. Where municipalities are struggling even to collect waste, disposal inevitably receives less attention.

- Most municipalities have no experience of controlled disposal. They may identify disposal sites but few actively manage them.

- Contracting out waste services has been suggested as a solution to low municipal capacity, but there are many uncertainties surrounding the issue: in what manner should the service be privatised? Should a large or small contractor be used? Can the municipality supervise and monitor the contract?

2. Political commitment

- Solid waste management is much more than a technical issue; it has implications for local taxation, employment, regulation, and any changes need political support to be effective. Unfortunately, it is rarely a priority for political leaders unless there is strong and active public interest. Thus there is little incentive to invest in disposal or control unofficial practices.

- Many people rely on waste picking for their income and a controlled disposal operation could be seriously disrupted if the practice was allowed to continue. Banning picking, however, requires strong management and political commitment.

- There are many unofficial practices (such as fuel theft) which would be threatened by the introduction of a controlled operation, making staff unwilling to co-operate.

3. Finance and cost recovery

- Development of a sanitary landfill site represents a major investment and it may be difficult to give it priority over other resource demands.

- The need for funding can make municipalities dependent on donors or loan agencies that apply pressure to reach high, possibly unachievable, standards of disposal.

- Finance may be available in the short term for establishment of a disposal site, but reliable revenue is needed for long-term recurrent costs. This is very hard to provide if residents are unwilling to pay taxes for waste disposal.

4. Technical guidelines

■ Standards from high income countries may be not appropriate in low income countries due to differences in climate, resources, institutions etc. However, relatively little appropriate guidance is available for low income countries.

■ A lack of accurate data — or the means of getting it, compounds planning problems. For example, it may not be possible to undertake a geophysical survey of a disposal site or even make an accurate estimate of the total daily generation of domestic waste.

■ Due to these uncertainties, officials find themselves ill-equipped to plan a disposal operation which is both achievable and avoids unacceptable environmental hazards. They may try to adopt unsuitable, highly expensive western designs or ignore the issue altogether, perhaps fearing prohibitive costs.

5. Institutional roles and responsibilities

■ A disposal site may be located outside the boundary of the town it serves, and may serve more than one town. This necessitates the co-ordination of all authorities concerned and may involve departments that are accustomed to acting independently.

■ Within authorities, the roles and responsibilities of different departments need to be clearly defined and accepted by all concerned. Some smaller towns may not have staff with specific responsibility for providing a solid waste management service.

6. Location

■ The accessibility of a disposal site — especially its distance from town — is an important factor in site selection, especially when staff and the public do not have a strong incentive to use it when compared with indiscriminate dumping.

Common practices

The cities visited during the research may well typify solid waste management arrangements in low income countries. Reliable data is notoriously hard to obtain, making it difficult to make comparisons between different places, two common features are:

■ The amount of waste collected by municipalities is markedly less than that generated at source by households, commerce and industry.

■ Users are not satisfied with the standard of service they receive.

Table 1. The cities at a glance	
City	*Waste disposal*
Karachi ■ Population 8.5 million ■ 6,000 tonnes of domestic waste daily	■ Uncontrolled disposal at 20 different places outside the city limits, some are large, with one receiving about 1000 tonnes daily. ■ The official municipal dump site is full. ■ Two new sites are at the planning stage. ■ Over 30% of municipal expenditure is on solid waste management.
Faisalabad ■ Population 2.5 million ■ 800 tonnes waste daily	■ Uncontrolled disposal on one major site and 2 to 3 small sites. ■ The municipal authority has recently acquired a 9 hectare site for disposal. ■ There is no disposal at the acquired site as yet.
Addis Ababa ■ Population 1.8 million ■ 300 tonnes waste daily	■ Uncontrolled disposal of officially collected waste on a 25 hectare site located at Rappi, 12.5km from the centre of the city. ■ The site has been in operation for the last 33 years.
Arba Minch ■ Population 37,000 ■ Waste generation unknown	■ There is no mechanism for waste collection or pattern of disposal for this small town.

Existing disposal practices vary from city to city and country to country. However, improvement to waste disposal is often a gradual process, as it receives much lower priority than waste collection and transportation. Table 2 identifies a range of on-going disposal practices from the least to the most developed, with characteristic indicators for each. Understanding where a town currently lies on this scale is a useful first step in assessing how much improvement is viable.

Table 2. Solid waste disposal practices in low income countries		
Status	**Description**	**Indicators**
Waste discarded at source	This is common in cities and towns where no collection system operates. Waste is deposited by households in streets and open spaces as they generate it.	■ No primary collection. ■ No functional institution responsible for solid waste management. ■ Scattered waste in streets and open areas. ■ Waste consumption by animals is common. ■ Burning of piles of waste.
Uncontrolled local disposal	There is a primary collection system and waste is taken manually or in carts to a few disposal points. There is no secondary transportation using vehicles. Such systems are common in small towns.	■ There is institutional responsibility for solid waste management. ■ Waste is removed from streets to nearby open places. ■ Waste quantities accumulate. ■ Waste picking starts. ■ Waste consumption by animals is common.
Uncontrolled city disposal	Primary and secondary collection is available. Waste is generally removed from the immediate environment and taken in vehicles to un-designated places away from residential areas.	■ There is an institution responsible for solid waste management. ■ Waste is removed in two stages i.e. primary and secondary. ■ Transfer points are provided. ■ Often, vehicle drivers decide which disposal point to use. ■ Waste picking continues at all stages.
Semi-controlled disposal	Primary and secondary collection is provided. Waste is generally removed from the immediate environment and taken in vehicles to designated places outside the residential area. There is no management or equipment at the disposal site.	■ Waste disposal options are in the planning stage. ■ Vehicle drivers transport the collected waste to designated sites. ■ Waste picking continues at all stages.
Controlled disposal	Primary and secondary collection provided. Waste is generally taken outside the residential area to designated sites in vehicles. There is some operational control and equipment / plant available at the site, though disposal is not fully engineered.	■ Engineered disposal options are in the planning stage. ■ Vehicle drivers transport the collected waste to designated sites. ■ Controls over waste picking at disposal site begins. ■ Solid waste authority owns the site. ■ Waste picking continues.
Fully engineered disposal	Waste is disposed of in a fully-controlled manner with maximum protection to the environment. This is quite uncommon in low income countries.	■ Details of planning and records are available. ■ No waste picking.

Waste disposal options

The poor practices of waste disposal could be improved through a range of options. An introduction to and comparison of the range of disposal options is set out below.

Non-engineered disposal

This term refers to all of the practices listed in Table 2, apart from fully engineered disposal. In low income countries, the most common disposal systems are those without any control, or with only slight or moderate controls. They tend to remain in place for many years since engineered disposal requires capital expenditure, a reliable revenue stream and effective primary and secondary collection. The environmental cost of this situation could be high and include fly, mosquito and rodent breeding, water pollution, air pollution from odour and smoke, and degradation of land. This can create a public impression that all land disposal is offensive, leading officials to search for expensive alternatives such as incineration (Coad, 1995).

With some basic site operations like spreading, compacting and covering, the waste may be contained and some environmental health control may be achieved over burning, fly breeding and waste picking. However, environmental hazards from leachate and gases will remain if the site is not properly engineered and managed.

Sanitary landfilling

Box 3. What is sanitary landfilling?

Sanitary landfill is a fully engineered disposal option. It avoids the harmful effects of uncontrolled dumping by spreading, compacting and covering the waste on land that has been carefully engineered before use. Through careful site selection, preparation and management, operators can minimise risks from leachate and gas production both in the present and the future. Site design and plans consider not only waste disposal but after-care and ultimate land use once the site closes (Figure 1).

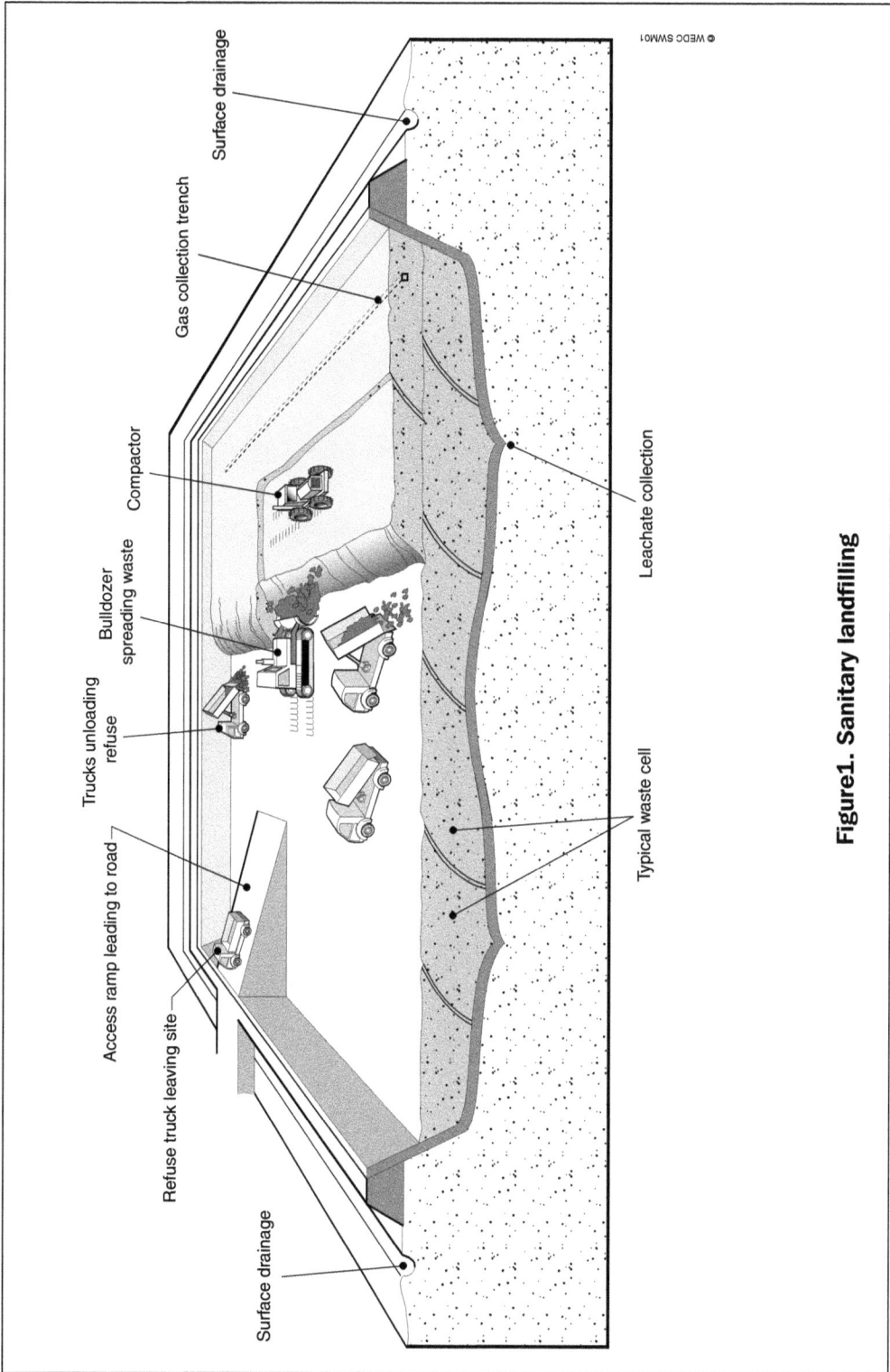

Figure1. Sanitary landfilling

The hazards arising from landfill can vary from one site to another but depend primarily on a range of factors including waste composition, moisture, and climate. As a guideline, sanitary landfilling should meet the minimum requirements set out below:

Box 4. Minimum requirements for sanitary landfilling

Location

- Careful siting to minimise groundwater and other potential pollution problems.

- Ideally sited away from present and proposed residential areas but not to the extent that transport costs become un-affordable.

- Adequate barriers to protect nearby residents where present.

- Control of wind blown litter (paper, plastics etc.) by screens and cover.

Operation

- Minimise contact between waste and water.

- Compaction of refuse and covering to prevent nuisance through flies and vermin.

- Prevent the formation of pools of water where mosquitoes could breed.

- Discourage rodents and enable early discovery of burrows through monitoring.

- Minimise smells and prevent burning by compacting and covering refuse and controlling site operations.

- Fill depressions so that profile is uniform.

- Control birds through prompt coverage of waste.

Management and control

- Make site ownership and responsibility clearly identified.

- Earmark site officially and ensure it is actually used by persons allowed at the site.

- Actively monitor and control site operations.

- Restore the site to an acceptable condition after closure.

- Plan for future use of the site.

Sanitary landfilling is one of the most effective and simple-to-operate disposal options. As such, it is likely to be applicable to many locations, provided the capital and revenue costs can be met. Section 5 of this report provides a review of landfill guidelines appropriate to countries facing the constraints identified in Box 2 earlier.

Box 5. When sanitary landfilling is suitable

Sanitary landfilling is a recommended disposal option for developing countries when suitable land is available at an affordable price. This option must be considered after an assurance that pollution could be controlled and human and technical resources are available to operate and manage the site.

Composting

Box 6. What is composting?

Composting is an *aerobic* process that converts waste into a humus-like material through microbial action on the *organic portion* of the solid waste. If carried out effectively, the final product is stable, odour-free, does not attract flies and can act as a soil conditioner.

Compost is mainly used as a soil conditioner to increase organic content, water retention and improve soil structure. The addition of compost to soil can make it more resistant to wind and water erosion, can retain more water, and make it easier to till. Compost also provides small quantities of inorganic and other trace nutrients. It improves the usefulness of artificial fertilisers by holding them in the soil, enabling the plants to benefit from them over a longer period.

The simplest method of composting is to place the waste in a long pile (known as a windrow) and aerate it by turning at intervals (initially every few days). Material in the warmer centre of the windrow matures faster; turning moves it to the outside, while cooler outer material which still contains pathogens and fly larvae moves to the middle.

If large quantities of waste are to be composted, special plant and equipment are needed. This may include:

- machinery for turning the windrows;

- systems of pipes and blowers or vacuum pumps to blow or draw air through the windrows (static aeration); and

- large rotating cylinders, or tower digesters, in which the waste is aerated and turned as it progressively falls down.

For most developing countries, windrow construction is likely to be the most appropriate. The rate of decomposition of organic material and the quality of the end product can be improved by introducing earthworms — a system known as vermi-composting. The worms eat waste and produce a cast (natural waste product) with a content of nitrogen, phosphorus and magnesium several times that of soil, making it a good soil conditioner. Vermiculture can be carried out on a small scale but the process demands careful control. When considering it as a disposal option, local pilot studies may be very useful.

Compost is not a complete disposal option as it produces a bi-product. A major drawback of composting is that there may be no demand for the product. While agricultural use necessitates large quantities (20 to 100 tonnes per hectare per year), the transportation costs can be considerable and in many soils a greater short-term return can be achieved by investing the same money on artificial fertiliser. Furthermore, some wastes are not suitable for composting due to contamination, including a high heavy metal content for example, printed paper or sludge from wastewater treatment.

To date, large scale composting has rarely succeeded in low income countries. If this option is considered, detailed studies should be undertaken on waste composition, the market for compost, appropriate systems and operation and maintenance requirements before making a decision to go ahead.

Box 7. When composting is suitable

Composting can be considered as a disposal option when biodegradable waste is available and there is a use or market for the bi-product. Large-scale composting should only be undertaken if adequate skilled manpower and equipment are available.

Incineration

> ### Box 8. What is incineration?
>
> Incineration is the controlled burning of waste in a purpose built facility. The process sterilises and stabilises the waste and for most wastes, will reduce its volume to less than a quarter of the original. Most of the combustible material is converted into carbon dioxide.

An incineration plant comprises of a waste receiving and charging (feeding) area, a furnace, residue handling facilities, and gas cleaning facilities. Ideally, it should be designed to recover the energy released by combustion though this may not be feasible for small-scale incineration, for example, of healthcare waste which provides a means of sterilising hazardous material.

Controlled burning is often seen as a modern and hygienic treatment option, but in practice it can be unreliable, polluting and expensive for low-income countries. This may result from poor plant design; inadequate infrastructure; lack of operation and maintenance skills; high capital and operating costs; unsuitable waste characteristics; and, the relatively low cost of sanitary landfilling.

Unsuitable waste composition is often a major drawback in developing countries where waste reaching the furnace typically has a high content of inert material in the form of silt and dust from street sweepings, and a low proportion of paper and plastics after waste picking. Even if it has a high organic content, much of the organic material has a high water content (such as vegetable waste) and is less suitable for burning than paper-based waste. An extensive waste sampling programme in India, for example (Bhide and Sunaresan, 1984) found that most of the waste had a calorific value of just 3350 joules/g compared with 9200 joules/g in high income countries. A similar picture emerges in Table 3 which compares key waste characteristics in the four case study cities with those in developed countries. Note that waste in the former has a high proportion of ash and fines.

Table 3. Comparison of typical waste composition in case study areas and high income countries

Characteristics	Case study cities*	High income countries**	Comments
Paper	1 to 4%	20 to 50%	Low paper content indicates low calorific value.
Plastics	1 to 6%	5 to 10%	Plastic is low as compared to high income countries though the use of plastics has increased in developing countries in recent decades.
Ash and Fines	17 to 62%	3 to 10%	Ash and fines do not contribute to combustion process.
Moisture Content	30% to 40%	15 to 30%	Moisture contents depend largely on the nature of the waste, climate and collection frequency. Waste can dry out while awaiting collection.
Bulk Density	300kg/cu-m to 400g/cu-m	150kg/cu-m	Heavier waste may cost more to handle and be difficult to burn.

* Ranges of data collected from Karachi, Faisalabad, Addis Ababa and Arba Minch.

** Data reported in Bhide and Sundaresan, 1984.

As a result of these problems, the incineration of municipal solid waste is only cost effective in regions where suitable sites for landfilling are scarce (UNEP, 1996) and where other factors are favourable.

Box 9. When incineration is suitable

Incineration should only be used as a disposal option when landfilling is not possible and the waste is high in combustibles such as paper or plastics. It is essential that appropriate infrastructure, skilled manpower and technology are available to operate and maintain the plant and equipment.

Gasification, refuse derived fuel and pyrolysis

Gasification is the partial oxidation of carbonaceous material through combustion at high temperatures (roughly 1000°C) to single carbon molecules, forming a gas which is mainly carbon dioxide, carbon monoxide, hydrogen, water and methane. The gas is used as a fuel.

Refuse Derived Fuel (RDF) is the name given to the combustible part of raw waste if it is separated for the purpose of burning as a fuel. Various physical processes such as screening, size reduction, magnetic separation etc. can be used to separate the combustibles, resulting in RDF with typical heating values of 12000 to 16000 joules per gram. The process is relatively expensive.

Pyrolysis is the thermal degradation of carbonaceous material to gaseous, liquid and solid fractions by heat in the absence of oxygen. This occurs at temperatures between 200 and 900°C. The product of pyrolysis is gas of the relatively high calorific value of 20,000 joules per gram with oils and tars and a solid burned residue. Each of these components may be used as a fuel and the ratio of each is dependent upon the particular pyrolysis process used.

Box 10. When other technologies are suitable

Technologically the above processes present efficient waste treatment alternatives to incineration. However, they do not provide complete disposal options for the large quantities of waste in low income countries or waste of varying composition. High capital and operating costs and the need for skilled manpower also make them unsuitable at the present time. Further research is needed to make the above processes more appropriate to low income countries.

Summary

A brief summary of disposal options and their suitability for low income countries is given in Table 4. It is clear from this that sanitary landfilling will in many cases be the most appropriate (perhaps the only) safe option for waste disposal.

Table 4. Summary of waste treatment and disposal options

Disposal option	Description	Application in low income countries
Uncontrolled dumping	Waste is dumped at a designated site without any environmental control measures.	A very common but unsatisfactory option, which poses health risks and causes environmental problems.
Sanitary Landfilling	Controlled application of waste on land.	Low cost and low technology solution when land is available. Presents some hazards if poorly operated (e.g. pollution by leachate).
Composting	Biological decomposition of organic matter in waste under controlled conditions.	Requires sufficient proportion of bio-degradable material in the waste. Not a complete disposal system; if there is no market for compost a further disposal option will still be needed. Large centralised schemes have not been successful.
Incineration	The controlled burning of waste at high temperature to reduce its volume. Plant is designed to recover the energy released by combustion.	High capital cost, requires highly skilled operation and control. The waste must have a high calorific value, which may not exist in low and middle income countries. Cost-effective only if landfill sites are not available.
Gasification	Decomposition of organic matter in waste under controlled conditions to obtain methane and other gases for use as fuel.	High cost and technologically complicated for developing countries.
Refuse Derived Fuel	Separation of combustible materials from solid waste for use as fuel.	Depends on the presence of combustible material in the waste. Expensive and therefore of limited use in developing countries.
Pyrolysis	High temperature conversion of organic materials in the absence of oxygen to obtain combustible by-products.	Capital intensive with high running costs. Technically complex; the full operational and cost issues are not widely known.

Section 3

Selection of Disposal Options

The framework

This section presents a framework which can be used to select appropriate options for municipal waste disposal in low income countries. It is based on a list of five desirable features of a waste disposal system, as listed below. The available options can be assessed in terms of their effectiveness with regards to these features.

Box 11. Desirable features of a waste disposal system

Technical	Efficient and effective operation of the technology used
Institutional	Ability and willingness of local agency to operate and manage the system
Financial	Ability to finance the implementation, operation and maintenance of the system
Social	No adverse social impacts
Environmental	Positive environmental impact

For each of these features, the framework lists a range of issues and questions in order to assess whether a treatment or disposal option meets the requirements. The issues are explored in more detail in a series of sub-frameworks. Note that:

■ The framework explores not only technical but also institutional, financial, social and environmental aspects of waste disposal. Technical considerations must not override other concerns.

- The framework is an aid to the decision making-process and helps to ensure that key issues have been considered. The bibliography can be used to obtain further detailed investigations.

- Some issues can be assessed in a general sense (for example the high costs of certain technologies), but the answers to many questions will depend on the specific local situation. It is not possible, therefore, to say that any one option will always be the most appropriate.

- The sub-frameworks explain how and why the necessary information should be obtained.

- An appraisal of waste disposal options using this framework needs to be carried out by a team with expertise in the five areas listed.

Section 4 demonstrates the application of the framework by using it to select an appropriate waste disposal option for the case study city of Karachi.

Photograph 1: Uncontrolled dumping and burning of waste.

Box 12. Framework for selection of waste disposal options

Desirable feature   **Issues and questions to address**

1. Technical
Efficient and effective operation of the technology used

Composition of waste
- Waste composition and quantity.

Existing practises
- Current collection and transportation system.
- Local recycling practices.

Siting
- Locations for potential treatment/disposal sites.
- Availability of engineering materials (e.g. soils).

Technology
- Secondary data on local climate, water resources and geology/hydrogeology.
- Nature of plant and equipment required.
- Operation and maintenance requirements of plant and equipment.
- Local, regional and national experience with different technologies and systems.
- Potential to scale up and replicate disposal options which have been run as local pilot projects.
- Supporting infrastructure for waste collection, transfer and haulage.
- Availability of technical support (locally or nationally).
- Technical assessment of potential options.

Other
- Anticipated by-products and requirements for their disposal or treatment.

2. Institutional
Ability and willingness of responsible agencies to operate and manage the system

Structures, roles and responsibilities
- Current institutional framework for waste management, including roles, activities and responsibilities.
- Existing plans for improving solid waste systems.

Operational capacity
- Municipal capacity for regulation and monitoring of operations.
- Local experience in managing different technologies.
- Scope for providing the necessary staff training.

Incentives
- Incentives to improve management and practices of waste disposal.
- Local support for better waste management.

Innovations and partnerships ■ Scope for different contracting options including private sector involvement.
■ Opportunities for partnerships with other agencies, departments or organisations for service delivery.

3. Financial
Ability to finance the implementation, operation and maintenance of the system
Financing and cost recovery ■ Capital and recurrent costs of the options.
■ Current revenue and expenditure on waste management.
■ Likely need for external finance for capital costs.
■ Willingness to raise finance for improved waste management.
■ Access to loan or grant assistance.
■ Ability to service capital loans.
■ Mechanisms for financing recurrent costs.

4: Social
No adverse social impact

Waste picking
■ Extent of waste picking at the existing dump sites.
■ Potential impact on livelihood of waste pickers.
■ Arrangements for waste picking in the proposed system.
■ Options for maintaining access for waste pickers at disposal site.

Other
■ Health and income implications for the poor.
■ Public opinion on the existing and proposed system.
■ Public pressure to develop improved disposal facilities.
■ Potential for creating more livelihood opportunities through developing new disposal options.

5: Environmental
Positive environmental impact

Initial environmental risks
■ An assessment of adverse impact of existing disposal option.
■ Anticipated impact of proposed disposal option(s).
■ Associated hazards and risks to nearby population, resources and workers.

Long-term environmental risks
■ Long-term implications (future generations).
■ Options to close down disposal options at the end of their useful life.
■ After care upon closing down.

The sub-frameworks

The issues listed in the framework are further expanded as a series of questions in the sub-frameworks. Each question has three components:

- What information/data is required?

- Why do we need the above data/information?

- Where are the possible sources of the above data/information?

Technical

Composition of waste

What is the composition and quantity of waste? What are other waste characteristics such as density, moisture content etc.?
- What is the wet weight percentage of the different components (e.g. paper, cardboard, plastics, metals, organic matter, silt) present in the waste?

- What is the approximate total daily generation of each type (municipal, hazardous and hospital) of waste?

Why do we need the above data/information?
The nature of the waste influences its pollution potential and hence affects engineering design and management. It also has an impact on collection and transport, and the potential for recycling. In the case of landfilling, the quantities of waste are required to decide the size and the scale of operation.

Where are the possible sources of the above data/information?
- Look for secondary information sources for example, local studies conducted in the past.

- Verify and validate the available data through judgement and additional testing.

- Quantities of waste could be assessed on a limited scale by weighing the waste as it is collected by waste collectors or by weighing the vehicles if a house to house collection system is operating.

■ Composition of waste could be assessed by separating various components from a sample of mixed waste.

While estimating or validating the waste composition and quantities, it is important to carefully select the sampling point, since the waste characteristics in low income countries may change significantly between various stages from generation to disposal. Waste compositions and generations also vary from season to season and from one income area to another.

Existing practices

How are collection and transportation practices currently organised? How do they affect waste composition?
■ How is the waste collected and transported?

■ What is the frequency of the service?

■ How reliable is the service in various income groups?

■ How do the current collection practices affect the waste properties? For example, compacting vehicles could increase the waste density.

Why do we need the above data/information?
Collection and transportation practices may have an impact on the nature of waste. For example, delays in waste transportation could lead to a loss in moisture. Street sweepings from unpaved streets could increase the quantities of silt and dust. It is important to understand the current and proposed systems of waste collection and transportation. At the same time, factors such as waste density will affect the choice of transport system. All these practises could have significant effects on planning, design and operations of disposal facilities.

Where are the possible sources of the above data/information?
■ Work studies and observations to understand the current system.

■ Forecast changes in waste properties with changes in collection and transportation.

■ Cross check with the secondary information sources for example, local studies conducted in the past.

What are current recycling practices — formal and informal?
How do they affect waste properties? How would they affect the proposed treatment/disposal options?
- What is the extent of recycling activity?

- How it is organised both, formally and informally?

- What materials are separated?

- What quantities of materials are separated?

- How many people are involved?

Why do we need the above data/information?
Recycling by the informal sector is common in all low income countries. Resaleable waste components are separated at different stages of the waste management system. These practices may result in changes in waste composition. For example, if lighter components such as paper, plastics and cardboard are separated, the remaining waste may be high in density and low in calorific value.

Where are the possible sources of the above data/information?
- Secondary information, past studies and observations.

- More focused studies on recycling patterns and their impact.

- Waste sampling at different stages to assess the impact of recycling on waste composition and quantities.

- Studies conducted from social development perspectives.

Siting

Where could treatment/disposal sites be located?
- What is the distance of potential sites from collection areas?

- What are the traffic and other road conditions between the collection area and the disposal sites and their impact on collection efficiency?

- What is the volumetric capacity of the available site (if it is for a landfill)?

- What are the geotechnics of proposed site, i.e. soil type, permeability, location of water resources, their quality and movement?

- What are the present and proposed future land-uses of site and surrounding area?

- What is the cost of land?

- What is the ownership of land?

Why do we need the above data/information?
In the case of landfilling, selecting a site with appropriate geology can, with a supporting risk assessment, alleviate the need for expensive control measures. However, other factors must also be considered in order to design an effective integrated waste management system, i.e. transportation must not be too costly (in time or money) to be carried out successfully. The present land-use of the site is important as relocation of the present activities may be needed and the land-use in the surrounding area of the waste disposal site must be known due to possible impact on/by those activities.

Where are the possible sources of the above data/information?
- Geotechnical investigations of proposed site and validation through spot tests.

- Maps/surveys of surrounding area.

- Survey of routes from collection area to disposal sites.

- Additional investigations.

What is the availability of engineering materials?
- Are the required materials for the construction and operation of waste disposal facility available?

Why do we need the above data/information?
The availability of engineering materials locally will have an effect on the viable options for waste disposal. Importing materials may increase the project cost.

Where are the possible sources of the above data/information?
- Ask local suppliers and construction firms.

- Investigate geotechnical data.

Technology

What is the local climate, water resources and geology/hydrology? How would these affect the design and operation of treatment/disposal options?
What would be the likely impact of the treatment/disposal option on environmental resources?

- What are the rainfall characteristics?

- What is the likely ground water flow of the site and at what depth?

- What are the average monthly temperatures?

- What are locations and size of water resources?

Why do we need the above data/information?
The choice of disposal option is likely to be influenced by the local climate etc. For example, if planning a landfill site the expected quantity of leachate must be calculated which is partially dependent on precipitation on the site. The ground water flow influences how the leachate disperses away from the site.

Where are the possible sources of the above data/information?
- Local meteorological data offices.

- Results of any previous geological surveys of the area.

- Previous bore hole records etc.

What plant and equipment would be required?
What would be its power, operation, maintenance and repair requirements?
- What operations need to be performed?

- What plant/equipment could be used to do this?

- What are the technical specifications for the plant/equipment?

Why do we need the above data/information?
In order to work out the requirements and hence ascertain whether it is possible to provide the needed power supply, operation, maintenance and repair facilities at the proposed locations.

Where are the possible sources of the above data/information?

- Detailed design documents/ specifications of various components at waste disposal facility.

- Plan of operations for the waste disposal options.

- Data from supplier and experience in other similar cities.

- Evaluation reports.

What local, regional or national experience is there with different technologies and systems?

- What waste disposal technologies have been attempted elsewhere in the country?

- Were the above successful? If not, why not?

- Have there been any successful local pilot projects? If so, what was learnt from them? Could they be replicated on a larger scale?

- Who are the key actors and stakeholders in local pilot projects? Are they initiatives of individuals? Are the municipalities fully involved?

- How are the pilot projects managed and financed?

- Have any lessons been incorporated into mainstream waste management activities?

Why do we need the above data/information?

The above information could help in planning a successful waste disposal facility as decisions could be made on the evidence of previous projects. It will highlight previous mistakes and successes so that they can be learnt from. It will also give an indication of where experience and technology presently exists in the waste disposal field and hence which options are most likely to be successful in the existing technical environment.

Where are the possible sources of the above data/information?

- Networking with other municipalities.

- Reports and journals.

- Professional/technical associations.

What supporting infrastructure is in place?
- Is the road network sufficient for proposed activities?

- How developed is the water, power supply and other infrastructure?

Why do we need the above data/information?
When planning any new development the ability of the surrounding infrastructure to supply/support the new venture must be checked. For example, if carrying waste by lorry to the disposal site, problems will be experienced if the roads are inadequate.

Where are the possible sources of the above data/information?
- Observation and studies.

What other technical support is available (locally or nationally)?
- Is there anyone else who can help?

Why do we need the above data/information?
There may be other technical help that is available in the country that can be useful. For example, people/organisations who have been involved in similar projects elsewhere.

Where are the possible sources of the above data/information?
- Both public and private sector associations.

- Local consultants.

- Local level umbrella organisations.

What are the technical advantages and disadvantages of each waste disposal option?
- Which option is technically the best?

Why do we need the above data/information?
In the assessment of which disposal option to use, it is necessary that the technical aspects of each option are discussed. It is likely that one or two options will show themselves to be 'technically' the best but the other selection categories may be decisive.

Where are the possible sources of the above data/information?
- Technical appraisal of all the options.

Other

What are the potential by-products of the operation and what are the requirements for their disposal?
- Will there be any by-products?

- Will the by-products be hazardous?

- How can they be disposed of?

Why do we need the above data/information?
There must be a plan to deal with any by-products that may be produced as they may be hazardous. In some cases a scheme will not be viable, or will have to be altered due to the nature or quantity of by-products produced e.g. if a non-engineered landfill produces a large quantity of leachate which would contaminate a potable water-supply a decision may be made to relocate the landfill or provide some protection of the water supply.

Where are the possible sources of the above data/information?
- Investigate previous projects with similar specifications.

- For a landfill site, analyse the components of waste at the disposal site, the expected precipitation etc. and calculate the expected leachate.

- To study the detailed design.

Institutional

Structures, roles and responsibilities

What is the current institutional framework for waste management, including roles, activities and responsibilities?

- What are the waste management activities carried out?

- Are the roles of solid waste management clearly defined?

- Who carries out each waste management activity?

- Who is responsible for the current solid waste management system?

Why do we need the above data/information?
It is important that an appreciation for the existing framework of waste management is gained in order that the correct people may be approached regarding new facilities. It is also necessary to get an insight into current practises and what works (and what doesn't) in order to know exactly what is needed.

Where are the possible sources of the above data/information?
- Define waste management activities from primary collection to disposal.

- Discuss with operational staff to clarify who does what. Identify responsibilities both within and between institutions (some responsibilities may be shared between departments).

Could the proposed disposal/treatment options fit in with existing arrangements?
- Would the option conflict with established arrangements?

- What are the existing plans for improving solid waste management?

- Would there be staff/a department available to manage it?

Why do we need the above data/information?
The new waste disposal scheme should fit in with existing operations or existing operations should be changed. Once the scheme is operating it is vital that it is run properly and efficiently.

Where are the possible sources of the above data/information?
- Discuss with operational staff.

- Find out if the staff have previous experience of similar responsibilities.

Operational capacity

What experience does the municipality have with the various options?
Will all necessary training be available for staff?
- Could the municipality control and monitor operations effectively?

Why do we need the above data/information?
If there is a large amount of local experience with similar schemes it is more likely that the scheme will work effectively. If there is no experience it may be necessary to provide extra training.

Where are the possible sources of the above data/information?
- Check previous experience with each of the options and availability of skilled, experienced personnel.
- Analyse training needs for the different options and how they could be met.
- Ascertain how the necessary technical and managerial skills could be obtained.
- Look at past performance in the regulation and control of waste management practices.

Incentives

Does the municipality have any real incentive to improve waste disposal practices?
- Is the municipality under external pressures from a regulator, funder, the public, or local groups?

Why do we need the above data/information?
If there is no real incentive to improve the waste disposal practises it is less likely that the municipality will be supportive of improvements. However, if they are under external pressure they are likely to be helpful. It will also be useful to see the reason for motivation of the municipality.

Where are the possible sources of the above data/information?

- Carry out research in the local area and ask members of the public representative organisation.

- An assessment of the past efforts.

What local political and administrative support is there for better waste management?

- What are the opinions of local political and administrative stakeholders on improving waste disposal?

- Would new proposals receive official support?

- Are there donors interested in financing improvements?

Why do we need the above data/information?

The above information would be very useful when attempting to improve the solid waste management in any place as it gives an idea of the opposition/support that may be met/given.

Where are the possible sources of the above data/information?

- Carry out research in the local area and employees of the municipality etc.

- Research NGOs acting locally.

- Research any similar previous projects undertaken/attempted in the area.

Innovation and partnerships

Will there be opportunities for new management arrangements which could improve operational efficiency?

- Does the municipality have experience of contracting out for the provision of urban services? Does this include setting terms of reference for maintenance?

- Are there other agencies, organisations or businesses that could provide services in partnership with the municipality?

- What is the extent of private sector involvement in the municipality as a whole?

■ Are there NGOs with suitable skills and capacity for delivering services?

Why do we need the above data/information?
It may be possible to use a new management technique that has not previously been used. All options must be investigated.

Where are the possible sources of the above data/information?

■ Carry out research in the local area and with the employees of the municipality.

■ Research NGOs acting locally.

■ Research any similar previous projects undertaken/attempted in the area.

Photograph 2: Survival on waste: A number of people earn their livelihoods through waste collection.

Financial

Financing and cost recovery

What are the capital and recurrent costs of the proposed options?
What is the current revenue and expenditure on waste management?
- What are the total costs involved in each of the proposed options?

- How much will the scheme cost to run?

Why do we need the above data/information?
It is vital that there is enough money to construct and run the scheme efficiently. It may be necessary to alter the proposed waste disposal option to reduce expenditure or to investigate other methods of financing operations.

Where are the possible sources of the above data/information?
- Data from another location where the same technology has been used.

- Clarify municipal expenditure and budget lines relating to waste management.

- Determine the local accounting basis for costs of waste management.

- Analyse accounts for actual and budgeted expenditure on waste management in recent years.

Would external finance be needed? Is the municipality willing to raise the finance for improved waste management?

Why do we need the above data/information?
If the municipality cannot finance the capital costs of the project either they must raise the money or an alternative funding route must be found.

Where are the possible sources of the above data/information?
- Assess general financial position in relation to own revenue and transfer payments.

- Analyse budgeted and actual funding of municipal capital works.

- Identify current mechanisms for financing capital works.

- Ask the opinions of local political and administrative stakeholders on financing improved waste disposal.

Does the municipality have access to loan or grant assistance? Could the municipality service capital loans? How could recurrent costs be financed?

Why do we need the above data/information?
It is important that the long term financing of the project is assessed.

Where are the possible sources of the above data/information?
- Analyse current externally financed capital projects.

- Identify potential sources of external funding, both in-country and international.

- Check eligibility requirements for different sources of external finance.

- Assess the impact of current projects on recurrent budgets.

- Compare indicative recurrent costs with own-revenue expenditure.

- Compare budgeted and actual expenditure on infrastructure operations and maintenance, including payments to utilities.

- Investigate options for raising additional revenue through general taxation and specific fees for waste treatment/disposal.

Photograph 3: Free Access: Waste pickers sorting waste as it is disposed of on a disposal site in a low income city.

34

Social

Waste picking

What is the extent of waste picking at dump sites?
- How many families benefit from activities at the existing waste disposal sites?
- How much does each family benefit, i.e. is it their sole income?

Why do we need the above data/information?
It is necessary to know how many people the proposed changes will effect in order to make informed decisions about the weight to be attached to such groups.

Where are the possible sources of the above data/information?
- Survey of existing waste picking practises.
- Past studies.

What would be the impact of proposed options on the livelihood of waste pickers at dump sites?
- How will the proposed options affect the number and location of waste disposal sites?
- What operational changes in the handling of waste will occur at the disposal sites?
- How far would the proposed option(s) reduce the number of pickers having access to waste?
- Which options maximise access to waste by waste pickers?

Why do we need the above data/information?
The extent to which the waste pickers are affected must be calculated.

Where are the possible sources of the above data/information?
- Carry out an assessment of the proposed waste disposal practises.
- Investigate alternative options for day-to-day disposal site operation in relation to providing access to waste.

Other

What would be the health and income implications for the poor (other than waste pickers)?

- Do the poor make money out of the existing waste practises? If so, how?

- Is there a link between the existing waste management practises and the health of the poor?

- How could/would the proposed scheme affect the above?

Why do we need the above data/information?

It is important to assess the positive and negative impacts of the various options on all sectors of the local population including the poorest of the poor. The direct impact of the management of solid waste on the poor is often hard to assess due to the fact that many health problems associated with bad waste management are also associated with poor living conditions.

Where are the possible sources of the above data/information?

- Carry out an assessment of how the various waste disposal options could reduce (or increase) the health risks posed to the poor through existing practices. For example, if sanitary waste is disposed of separately there would be less chance of contact with faecal matter either directly or indirectly.

- Interview local poor communities.

Are the general public aware of the need for better solid waste management? Are there active environmental pressure groups?

- What is the public opinion on the existing and proposed waste disposal systems?

- Is there any public pressure to develop improved disposal facilities?

Why do we need the above data/information?

If the general public are aware of the need for better solid waste management and the link between poor solid waste management and health, it is likely that they will support any ventures to improve the existing system. If the public are ignorant of this matter it may be necessary to conduct public training to ensure that the new system is supported and used effectively. Help in this may be obtained from environmental pressure groups.

Where are the possible sources of the above data/information?

■ Review past newspapers articles and news.

■ Open ended discussions with key informants.

■ Understand what NGOs are doing.

■ Interview local communities.

Is there any potential for creating more livelihood opportunities through developing new disposal options?

Why do we need the above data/information?

There may be an opportunity for job creation through the development of the new disposal option which may help the economy in the area grow. Urban areas in low income countries often have high rates of unemployment and therefore any new jobs will be met with much support.

Where are the possible sources of the above data/information?

■ Investigate similar projects elsewhere.

■ Study the disposal options in detail for possible job creation opportunities.

Photograph 4: Is it all over? Waste pickers sorting out waste at a disposal site after a refugees crisis.

Environmental

Initial environmental risks

Are effective environmental health controls in place? What are the negative impacts of current disposal practices? Would the proposed options reduce these negative impacts?

- What environmental regulations are there?

- Who enforces them?

- Are penalties invoked for non-compliance?

- Does the municipality have real power to influence waste disposal practices in the community?

- What are the likely environmental hazards and risks to the nearby population resources and workers of the proposed option?

Why do we need the above data/information?

It must be ensured that the proposed facilities will meet any environmental health controls. It is also necessary to know what controls exist so that they may be used to prompt compliance to any new disposal rules that will be in place with the new development. Environmental impact assessment of the proposed waste disposal schemes must be carried out. The positive and negative environmental health impacts of the new schemes (including the workers on the site and the local communities) must be compared to the current disposal practises.

Where are the possible sources of the above data/information?

- Ask municipality about environmental health controls.

- Study the impact of proposed waste disposal system on land, water and air.

- Interview residents to ask their perception of environmental problems regarding solid waste disposal.

- Investigate how the current system really operates on the ground.

Long-term environmental risks

What are the likely long-term environmental risks of the proposed scheme?

- What are the options to close down the disposal options at the end of their useful life?

- Is there a need for after care upon closing down?

Why do we need the above data/information?

Each option must be assessed in a holistic sense and thoughts about after care should not be left until the scheme is up and running. It may be that maintenance will be needed after the scheme has reached the end of its useful life. For example, in the case of a landfill site, maintenance may be needed to continue the recirculation of leachate.

Where are the possible sources of the above data/information?

- Examine the proposed design of the scheme in great detail and assess.

- Seek specialist advice from previous similar schemes.

Photograph 5: Red Signal Forever: A waste transportation scheme which operated for only a few days.

Section 4

Application of the Framework
Case Study: Karachi, Pakistan

Introduction

The purpose of this section is to demonstrate the application of the framework set out in Section 3 to a particular situation. Taking the city of Karachi, Pakistan as a case study it uses the five sub-frameworks (technical, institutional, financial, social and environmental) to identify a suitable waste disposal strategy. In this case, some of the factors considered have a much bigger influence than others on the final choice of system. In practice, the relative importance of the factors will vary from one situation to another and there is no universal 'best solution'.

Box 13. Background information about Karachi

With a population of 8.5 million, Karachi is Pakistan's largest city and its only port, being located on the country's southern coast.

Karachi Metropolitan Corporation (KMC) is responsible for waste collection and disposal in the city. The solid waste management department of KMC deals with planning and major procurement while operational responsibility rests with five District Management Offices (DMO's).

Municipal waste (domestic and commercial) is collected by sweepers (waste collectors), brought to transfer points, loaded into vehicles and transported for disposal. At present, there is no proper disposal facility in the city; instead, waste is taken outside the city limits and dumped on open land.

The following are key facts regarding solid waste management services in Karachi:

- Surveys indicate that users regard the solid waste system as inadequate.

- Only 70% of the waste generated is removed via municipal transportation.

- Neither the government nor NGO's have made a concerted effort towards waste reduction.

- A compost plant was installed in the early 1980's by a private company, but operated for only a few months before being abandoned.

- Transportation of waste by train to an out-of-town site was started in 1997 but abandoned after only a few days.

KMC is currently formulating plans for the development of landfill disposal sites. The Corporation has acquired two sites, each measuring 500 acres, to the south-west of the city. Funding is available for development of one site. Some access roads have been constructed to these sites through a loan obtained from The Asian Development Bank. In addition, KMC has obtained 100 acres of land from Karachi Development Authority (KDA) to the east of the city centre at Korangi.

Photograph 6: Lessons from the past: Uncontrolled dumping of waste for the past many years.

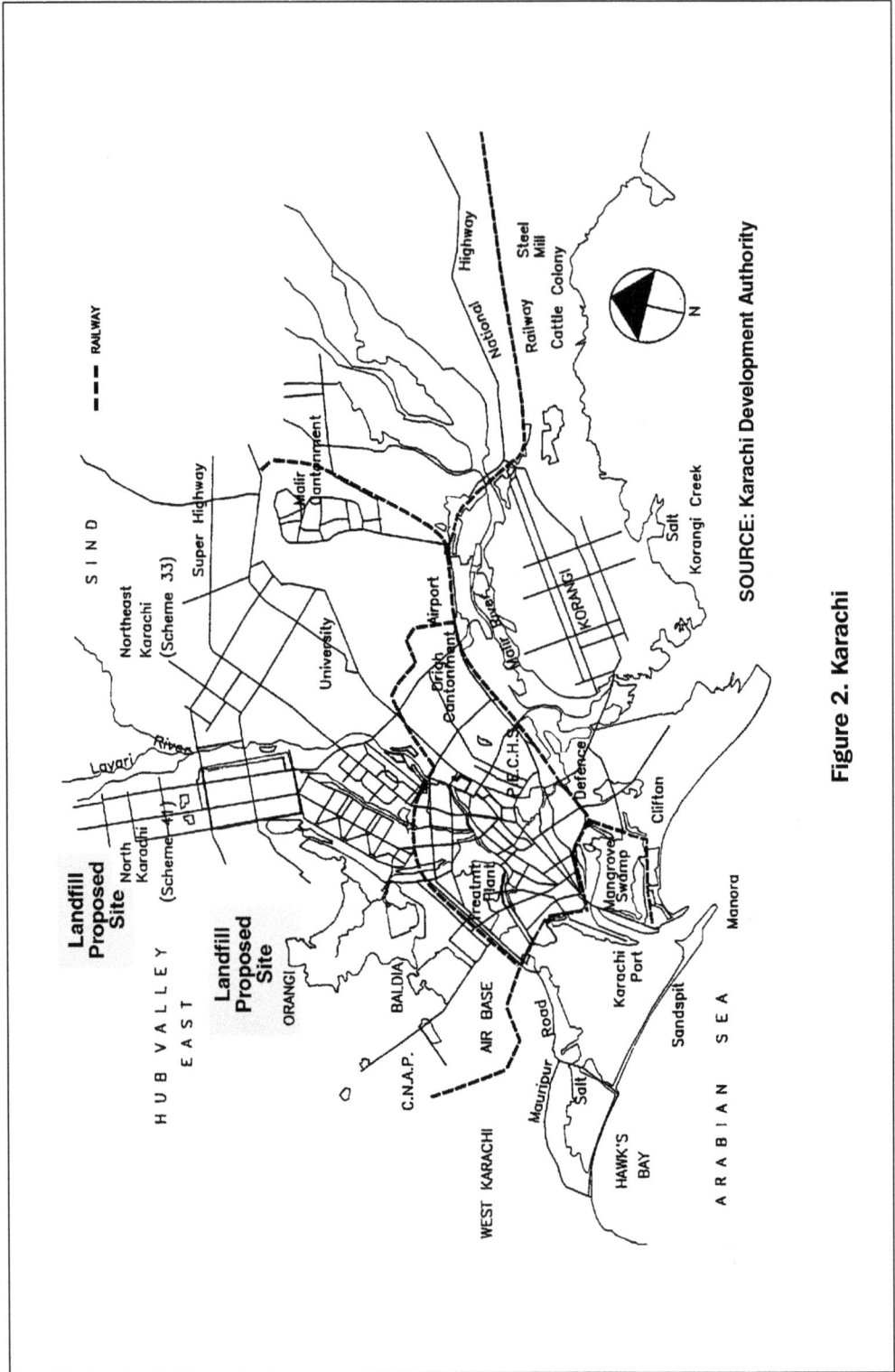

Figure 2. Karachi

SOURCE: Karachi Development Authority

Technical

Composition of the waste

What is the composition and quantity of waste? What are other waste characteristics such as density, moisture content, etc.?
Waste composition and quantity in Karachi varies by income group and with the seasons. Accurate data is difficult to obtain as most recent studies used an insufficient number of samples (i.e. less than 500 houses) but the consensus is that the city generates about 6000 tonnes of household waste daily. The per capita generation varies from 0.224 to 0.371 kg/ capita/ day (NESPAK, 1992). During collection and transportation, this waste undergoes a number of physical and chemical changes, including:

a) The removal of a large amount of saleable components such as paper, glass bottles, plastics etc.

b) The addition of street sweepings to the waste stream, which increases the quantity of inert materials such as dust, silt, clay etc.

c) Biodegradation and the loss of moisture due to the hot climate and an unreliable collection system which leaves waste in the open air for long periods.

Table 5 compares the results of a waste composition analysis at a Karachi disposal site with waste composition at source. It indicates that waste reaching the disposal sites contains a very high proportion of non-separable components such as dust and clay.

It is common for waste pickers to burn waste at the disposal site, leaving 50% of the total as un-burnt material. Field tests were conducted to measure the quantities of combustible organic materials at the disposal site. The waste was separated manually and the non-separable waste left was then burnt. It was found that the combustible portion is only 50% by weight of the total non-separable materials.

Bulk density also increases as the waste moves from collection to disposal. It has been reported as 150 to 200 kg/m^3 at source, increasing to 350 to 400 kg/ m^3 in vehicles and at final disposal sites. This increase is largely due to the removal of recyclables and the addition of street sweepings.

Table 5. Waste composition as percentage of wet weight at source and disposal sites			
Waste component	**At source [1]**	**At disposal site [2]**	**Comments**
Plastics	6.37%	6.9%	No picking of plastic (including plastic bags), helps in waste burning by pickers.
Paper and Cardboard	13.84%	2.0%	Waste picking removes much of this material.
Textiles	7.98%	6.9%	No picking.
Garden Waste	18.99%	Negligible	Animal scavenging at transfer points and disposal site.
Wood	0.25%	1.4%	
Ceramics, Clay, Stones etc.	10.55%	8.3%	
Rubber and Leather	1.58%	1.4%	
Food Waste	22.93%	11.0%	Reduction in moisture and through animal scavenging.
Metals	2.68%	Negligible	
Glass	2.62%	Negligible	
Non-separable	12.21%	62.1%	Bio-degradation and addition of street sweepings.

[1] NESPAK (1992) typical middle income area   [2] This study

Photograph 7: All re-saleable waste such as paper, plastics and cardboard is seperated before the waste reaches the disposal site.

Given the large quantities of waste needing disposal, the relatively low organic contents and calorific value and the high proportion of fines at the disposal end, landfilling appears to be preferable to other disposal options. Detailed studies should examine the potential for landfill gas and leachate generation to determine the required degree of engineering and pollution control. Separate collection of organic waste may facilitate effective composting and may contribute effectively in reducing landfill pollution potential. The relatively low calorific value will not support incineration.

Existing practises

How are waste collection and transportation currently organised? How do they affect waste composition?

The flow chart of waste collection and transportation system in Karachi is given in Figure 3. Irregular collection service in temperatures above 20°C leads to decomposition of organic waste and loss of moisture. The domestic waste is collected together with commercial, industrial and hospital waste. The waste is accessible to pickers who separate re-saleabale components such as paper, plastics, glass, bottles etc. Burning of waste and separation by waste may result in an increased proportion of inert elements, and corresponding reduction in calorific value.

Waste is exposed and accessible. The transportation is irregular in many areas, allowing picking and drying out. The reduction in paper and plastics reduces the combustible component of the waste at the disposal end, making it less suitable for incineration.

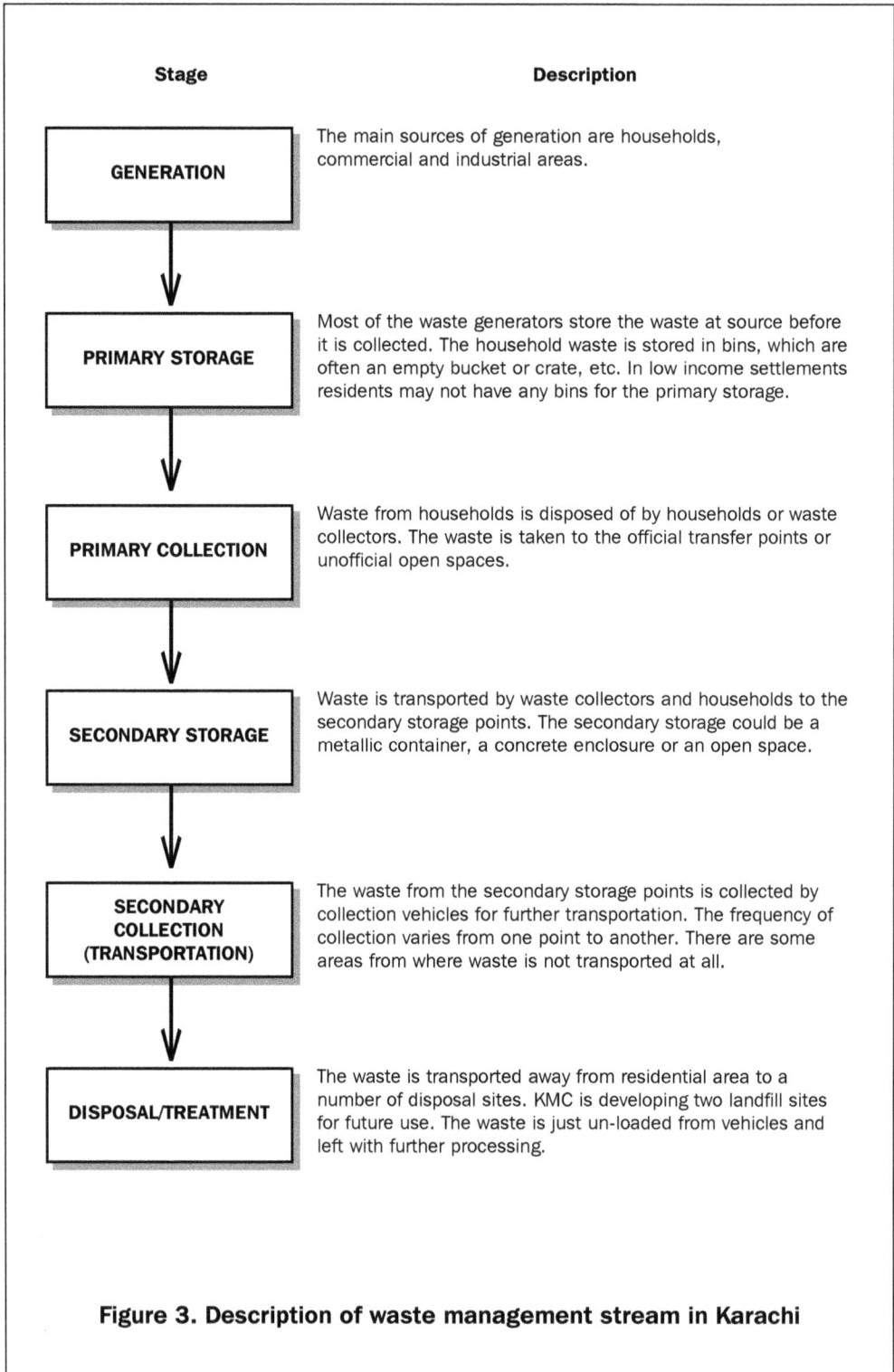

Stage	Description
GENERATION	The main sources of generation are households, commercial and industrial areas.
PRIMARY STORAGE	Most of the waste generators store the waste at source before it is collected. The household waste is stored in bins, which are often an empty bucket or crate, etc. In low income settlements residents may not have any bins for the primary storage.
PRIMARY COLLECTION	Waste from households is disposed of by households or waste collectors. The waste is taken to the official transfer points or unofficial open spaces.
SECONDARY STORAGE	Waste is transported by waste collectors and households to the secondary storage points. The secondary storage could be a metallic container, a concrete enclosure or an open space.
SECONDARY COLLECTION (TRANSPORTATION)	The waste from the secondary storage points is collected by collection vehicles for further transportation. The frequency of collection varies from one point to another. There are some areas from where waste is not transported at all.
DISPOSAL/TREATMENT	The waste is transported away from residential area to a number of disposal sites. KMC is developing two landfill sites for future use. The waste is just un-loaded from vehicles and left with further processing.

Figure 3. Description of waste management stream in Karachi

What are current recycling practices — formal and informal? How do they affect waste properties? How would they affect the proposed treatment/disposal options?

It is estimated that 15% of domestic waste (by wet weight) in Karachi is removed for recycling at household level, and a further 10% at transfer points. This practice provides employment or additional income for many people, though it is informal and takes place outside of official municipal procedures. The motivation for these operations comes from the thriving market for separated materials and the opportunity for additional income for householders. Table 6 gives a brief description of the complex network of actors involved in waste separation activities and where they occur in the solid waste management stream in Karachi.

Householders store re-saleable waste separately from other components and when a sizeable quantity has accumulated, sell it to itinerant waste buyers (IWB's) who roam the streets with push carts, donkey carts, bicycles or on foot. Payment is based on weight for each type of material though there is also a small group called 'barterers' who exchange waste for goods such as tea mugs, confectionery, kitchen utensils etc.

IWB's sell their goods to middle dealers, who also buy from households, shopkeepers and other sources and operate from permanent plots or shops. Middle dealers sell to main dealers (wholesalers) who buy single materials and have established contacts with recycling industries. Dealers in paper and ferrous metals generally operate on a large scale while plastic and glass operations are relatively small.

There is another category of dealers known as group leaders, who purchase only from street pickers. The material supplied by pickers is different and of a lower quality than that from itinerant waste buyers and is therefore traded by a different chain of operators.

More than 150 pickers — male and female — work at an unofficial disposal site to the south-west of Karachi which receives approximately 1000 tonnes of solid waste daily. The pickers work in separate groups and 'buy' waste from truck drivers for around Rs100 for three truckloads. In return, the drivers dump their waste in the area specified by the purchasing group. The waste is left to dry then burnt to enable the recovery of metals using magnets attached to pieces of wood (see photographs).

Table 6. Summary of actors and activities in the informal recycling process		
Stages	*Actors*	*Activities*
Source	Householders	Separate and store saleable waste components then sell to itinerant waste buyers.
Source	Domestic servants	Separate and store the saleable waste components in high-income areas then sell to itinerant waste buyers from low-income areas.
Source, primary collection	Sweepers	Collect waste from various sources, separate and sell saleable components during primary collection. The remaining waste is disposed of at transfer points or open plots.
Streets, transfer points	Street pickers	Separate saleable components in the street and at transfer points and sell to their group leaders or dealers.
Source	Itinerant waste buyers	Purchase separated waste from households and other sources and sell to middle dealers.
Source, streets and transfer points	Middle dealers	Purchase materials from itinerant buyers and sell to main dealers. Also process some materials to reduce transportation costs.
Source, streets and transfer points	Main dealers	Purchase bought waste from middle dealers and sell it to the recycling industry. Process and sometimes categorise materials for further transportation.
Source, streets and transfer points	Recycling industry	Convert waste materials to other saleable products.

Photograph 8: Another load of rubbish: A refuse truck load, waiting to be disposed of.

These practices are significant when considering potential treatment or disposal options because:

- They reduce the quantity of waste reaching the disposal site.

- By removing certain components, they alter the composition of waste at the disposal site. This reduces its suitability for certain treatment options, such as incineration or composting, and affects the ultimate pollution potential upon landfill.

- Waste picking activity at disposal sites could be extensive in future if the waste cannot be accessed by pickers in the streets or at transfer points.

> The separation of re-saleable items at the household level, during transportation and at final disposal provides livelihoods and valuable additional income for many poor people. Options which remove these opportunities should be avoided. Of all the disposal or treatment options, landfilling provides the greatest opportunity for the utilisation of re-saleable waste.

Siting

Where could treatment/disposal sites be located?
KMC have proposed two sites for waste disposal, at Korangi and Jam Chakro, which are 15 and 22km respectively from the city centre. The sites were acquired through a loan provided by the Asian Development Bank. The prime consideration in choosing the sites was ownership and availability. Municipal officials propose a transportation target of three trips (per vehicle) per day if fuel is not a constraint. Road access to both sites is fairly good although the road to Jam Chakro would need improvement to sustain the loads of full refuse trucks.

> The ownership and availability have been the major criteria in choosing the disposal sites in Karachi, however, given rapid city growth and the volume of traffic in the city centre, it would be advisable to develop disposal sites at three or four different locations outside the city limits.

Technology

What is the local climate, water resources and geology/hydrology? How would these factors affect the design and operation of treatment/disposal options?
There are several meteorological stations supplying climate data in Karachi. Daily and monthly temperatures average between 10.4°C and 30.2°C. However, from May to July the hottest months, the maximum day temperature often exceeds 35°C. Rainfall is quite low but occasionally very intense. Average annual rainfall is approximately 250mm with the wettest month in 20 years recording 319mm; 155mm is the heaviest recorded rainfall in one day.

The combination of high temperatures, sunshine and low rainfall has the following implications for waste disposal:

- Waste degrades rapidly and needs frequent collection.

- It dries en-route to the disposal site and may affect degradation in the landfill.

- Preliminary calculations using Christiansen's formula (see Figure 4) suggest that there is a negative water balance in Karachi. Therefore, if surface runoff is controlled through adequate drainage and compaction, there should be little or no leachate production, thus reducing pollution of the underground and surface water resources. The risk of chemical contamination could also be avoided if the landfill does not accept waste from industrial sources. This has potential significance for the design of the new site, but will require field testing to determine how much leachate is actually generated.

> High temperatures and low rainfall favour landfill over other disposal options, as it reduces the quantities of leachate generated.

What would be the likely impact of the treatment/disposal option on environmental resources?
The bulk of Karachi's water supply comes from the rivers Indus and Hub. There are also approximately 2,500 wells supplying about 8 million gallons of water per day where there is no mains supply, but this represents only 3% of the total. This groundwater suffers significant contamination — both chemical and bacteriological — and the future groundwater resources of the region

Karachi Lat 24° 54'

Months	E-T Rad	Mean M Temp	Ct	Mean RHm	Chm	Max sunshine hours	Mean sunshine hours	%	Cs	W (km/day)	Cw	Elev Ce for 30m	Pan Evap	Evap	Rainfall	R-E
Jan	304	10.4	0.6964	53	1.03	10.7	7.2	67.290	0.908	242.2416	1.303	0.973	118.618	83.033	8.1	-74.9329
Feb	323	20.4	1.0132	63	0.96	11.3	7.3	64.602	0.897	291.1344	1.368	0.973	176.873	123.811	8.5	-115.311
Mar	419	24.3	1.1432	66	0.93	12	7.3	60.833	0.875	342.2496	1.401	0.973	251.597	176.118	23.5	-152.618
Apr	455	27.7	1.2595	71	0.88	12.7	7.8	61.417	0.875	364.4736	1.401	0.973	284.196	198.937	4.8	-194.137
May	498	30.4	1.3534	72	0.87	13.3	9.1	68.421	0.92	451.1472	1.401	0.973	347.037	242.926	0	-242.926
Jun	490	31.1	1.3785	79	0.77	13.7	9.5	69.343	0.932	475.5936	1.401	0.973	313.363	219.354	1.5	-217.854
Jul	500	30.2	1.3462	83	0.71	13.5	7.4	54.815	0.854	356.47296	1.401	0.973	261.670	183.169	169.4	-13.7691
Aug	478	29.1	1.3075	85	0.67	13	7	53.846	0.844	400.032	1.401	0.973	227.536	159.275	15.7	-143.575
Sep	422	26.4	1.215	83	0.71	12.3	8.8	71.545	0.945	411.144	1.401	0.973	220.565	154.396	81.3	-73.0958
Oct	376	27.6	1.256	74	0.84	11.6	9.2	79.310	1	277.8	1.348	0.973	246.984	172.889	0	-172.889
Nov	307	24.3	1.1432	56	1.01	10.9	8	73.394	0.958	244.464	1.303	0.973	203.641	142.549	20.8	-121.749
Dec	283	19.5	0.9835	50	1.05	10.6	8.2	77.358	0.985	260.0208	1.327	0.973	175.135	122.595	40.9	-81.6947

Figure 4. Computation of Pan Evaporation by using Christiansen's Formula for Karachi

are at risk (Mohsin and Zubair, 1994). Given the low rainfall, it is probable that much of the pollution is caused by industrial activities, which may present a much higher risk than that associated with waste disposal.

The soils of Karachi are generally classified as coarse-grained ranging from sandy gravel, sand with gravel, to fine sand. The silt and clay content is generally low and in many cases negligible.

The soil structure of the two sites proposed by KMC is a mixture of gravel, sand and clay. The soil has been mainly transported by water and formation consists of limestone, sandstone and shale. The soil tests at a nearby site classified it as well graded gravel with sand.

Keeping in view the low reliance on groundwater sources and the negative water balance, as discussed, it may be concluded that the overall risk to underground and surface water resources from landfill leachate would be very low. The coarse soil may help in the removal of micro-organisms but not the salts and heavy metals should the leachate move.

> On the basis of the above, if landfilling were selected as a disposal option then the increased risk of pollution from leachate would be low. However, a more detailed investigation would be required to compare these risks with those from other disposal/treatment options and to look at the future potential impacts.

What plant and equipment would be required? What would be its power, operation, maintenance and repair requirements? What local, regional or national experience is there with different technologies and systems?
Typical landfill equipment/plant includes bulldozers, JCBs, excavators, back hoe and weighbridges. KMC have recently acquired 7 bulldozers, 2 sheep foot rollers and 2 back hoes for landfill operation (Javaid, 1997). The KMC's workshops is capable of maintaining refuse trucks but previous reports (Klundert, 1996 and NESPAK, 1992) have identified the lack of preventive vehicle maintenance as a major problem. Procedures for obtaining spare parts are time consuming, apparently to reduce pilferage and corruption, and this exacerbates the lack of maintenance. One study recommended gradual privatisation of repair and maintenance facilities.

Clearly, landfill plant and equipment could only be used efficiently if operation and maintenance systems are improved. Past performance also indicates that KMC would not be in a good position to adopt a treatment option employing complex technology, such as incineration. Even at national level, specialist resources are minimal.

> Municipal capacity to operate and maintain plant and equipment is limited. Of the options available, landfilling may be the most suitable because it employs the simplest technology and systems.

Have there been any successful local pilot projects? If so, what was learned from them? Could they be replicated on a larger scale?

KMC have carried out a pilot project on composting as a method of solid waste disposal. However, this project failed. KMC has no other experience of any safe disposal system, even on a pilot basis. Outside of government, there is no local experience of safe treatment or disposal apart from the use of incinerators at a few private hospitals. However, some NGOs are active in the initial stages of solid waste management such as community education, primary collection and recycling.

> Due to a lack of experience within KMC the option chosen should first be piloted at one site, to develop expertise which can be used for training other staff and eventual expansion.

What supporting infrastructure is in place?

The city of Karachi has a reasonable road network though there are repair and maintenance problems. It is also prone to both water and power shortages. Waste treatment/disposal designs that depend on power and water supplies may therefore face difficulties. For example, landfill using power for leachate re-circulation and a water supply for effective compaction.

Landfilling may be a suitable disposal option for Karachi as it needs minimum supporting infrastructure for its operation.

What other technical support is available (locally or nationally)?
Generally, there is a national shortage in Pakistan of qualified and experienced professionals in any aspect of solid waste management (ODA, 1994 and Klundert, 1996).

The planning and design of any future waste disposal operation will have to include careful human resource planning as many of the skills required are not locally available at present. Options requiring advanced and rare technical skills should be avoided, making landfilling the most viable option.

Institutional

Structures, roles and responsibilities

What is the current institutional framework for waste management, including roles, activities and responsibilities? Could the proposed disposal/treatment options fit in with existing arrangements?
Karachi Metropolitan Corporation (KMC) has a city-wide solid waste management department responsible for planning, landfilling, foreign aided projects and international procurement. The Corporation is also responsible for major administrative matters, financial allocations and the drafting and approval of local legislation.

In the past, KMC were directly responsible for waste collection, transportation and disposal but, following the division of the city into five operational zones, these tasks now come under the health departments of five District Management Offices, each headed by a Health Officer. The engineering departments of DMOs deal with the operation, repair and maintenance of motorised vehicles.

In addition to municipal operations, there a number of informal private operations in the city outside of government regulation and control. The most notable of these are waste recycling as discussed and the primary collection of waste by sweepers — some of them municipal staff undertaking private work. Both occur on a large scale and it may be neither possible nor desirable to stop them. Both could affect, or be affected by, the operation of possible disposal systems.

> While roles and responsibilities for solid waste management are well-defined, disposal sites are not currently staffed. Staff numbers are, however, high and it should be feasible to redeploy some personnel into treatment or disposal operations provided these did not require advanced technical skills. Landfilling would be the most viable option is this regard.

What experience does the municipality have with the various options? Will all necessary training be available for staff?

KMC has no experience of operating any safe waste disposal or treatment technology and currently lacks staff trained in solid waste management. The core group of technical personnel in the solid waste management department are mechanical and electrical engineers with good experience in procuring, maintaining and repairing waste collection vehicles but there is no expertise in waste management planning, economic appraisals or landfilling. The national experience of planning, designing and operating the sites is negligible. The capacity of KMC staff could be increased by external agencies and by experimenting with small scale landfilling. The private consultants could fill some of the capacity gaps.

> The lack of staff skilled in any method of safe disposal is a major constraint. Of the options available, landfilling would be the least difficult for KMC to learn to operate. Municipal capacity building should precede any new disposal operation.

Operational capacity

Could the municipality control and monitor operations effectively?
KMC lacks capacity in monitoring and controlling their current operations and there is no reason to believe that a new system would be run any better — unless they invested in improving the quality and efficiency of their work. Some treatments (such as incineration) can cause serious environmental problems if they are poorly operated or monitored. Composting can also cause pollution if poorly managed and inefficient operation will result in an undesirable product which then needs disposal.

> Due to low technical and managerial capacity, preference should be given to the simplest and most sustainable system available, in this case landfill.

Incentives

Does the municipality have any real incentive to improve waste disposal practices?
The obligation to provide a solid waste management service arises from the Local Government Ordinance (1979) which identifies 'sanitation' as a compulsory public health function of metropolitan and municipal corporations. Under this legislation:

> 'A corporation, municipal committee or town committee shall make adequate arrangements for the removal of refuse from all public streets, public latrines, urinals, drains and all buildings and lands vested in the council concerned and for the collection and proper disposal of such refuse'.

This is far from adequate to motivate municipalities to establish safe waste disposal facilities. The 1983 Environmental Ordinance created Pakistan Environmental Protection Agencies (PEPA) but these have so far been ineffective and there is no other regulatory body applying pressure on KMC to provide a better service. Generally, the country lacks appropriate institutions with staff skilled in environmental monitoring, evaluation, regulation and enforcement.

Karachi Metropolitan Corporation are under no pressure to enforce current laws and ordinances to improve waste disposal practice. This could lead to complacency in operating any new system and strengthens the case for the simplest possible disposal option.

What local political and administrative support is there for better waste management?

Political will is an important element in the development of solid waste management systems. Improvements in the solid waste service are usually visible and could create an immediate impact on the local environment. Solid waste management agencies are a major government employer in Karachi, with strong trade unions.

The local political environment of Karachi is, however, volatile and political will for developing safe waste disposal facilities is unstable. The political unstability has been a major constraint for long term infrastructure planning. The environmental and health problems arising from current disposal practices are not a priority concern for either the citizens or political parties in Karachi. This fact, plus the absence of enforceable legislation means that there is no real incentive for KMC to improve waste disposal, though it has been encouraged to do so by the Asian Development Bank (ADB), one of its major donors. With several areas in Karachi unable to secure a reliable waste collection system, disposal gets pushed even further down the list of priorities.

Lack of political commitment could threaten the long-term operation and monitoring of any waste treatment/disposal system. Options with high running costs would be particularly vulnerable to changes in municipal priorities. Disposal options need reliable operation and maintenance systems as they are central to the other stages. This needs a strong and sustainable political commitment.

Innovation and partnerships

Will there be opportunities for new management arrangements which could improve operational efficiency?

It is common practice in KMC to contract out parts of a project, such as detailed engineering design and construction to private sector. Should the proposed landfill sites go ahead, their planning, design and development will probably involve the private sector.

> The apparently positive attitude to private sector participation could enable KMC to compensate for a lack of in-house capacity, though their ability to supervise a privatised contract effectively — especially for a new and unfamiliar system — has not been proven.

Financial

Financing and cost recovery

What are the capital and recurrent costs of the proposed options?

For the option of landfilling the major cost component is land. At present there is a considerable area of state owned land available around Karachi. The process of transferring land to KMC takes time but the cost is minimal. In theory, if KMC transports all the current generation rate of 6000 tonnes/ day and compacted waste density of 500kg/ cu-m, KMC needs a net space of 4.5 million cubic meters per year. The topography of Karachi is generally flat and there are no abundant quarries etc. which could be used for waste disposal. If the waste is landfilled in a 3 meters deep prepared land, the cost of land at the market rate will be Rs7500 million for one year (please keep in mind that the annual health budget of KMC is around Rs500 million). Similarly the cost of operating the sanitary landfill will be Rs650 million per year. The cost of purchasing and operating waste incinerator and operating them is generally higher than sanitary landfilling.

Keeping in view the high cost of disposal options and minimum resources available with KMC, it may be concluded that KMC should gradually develop and plan the landfill sites. The need for affordable standards is further justified.

What is the current revenue and expenditure on solid waste management?

An analysis of municipal records reveals the financial management of solid waste management services and potential obstacles to securing safe disposal. KMC does not make any specific charges for its waste collection service; revenue comes mostly from the combined conservancy/sewerage charges collected by Karachi Water and Sewerage Board, based on property values assessed about 25 years ago. Cost recovery for these charges is very poor: in 1995, Rs141 million was billed but only half of it collected.

KMC spend money according to an annually published budget and set procedures. In 1996-7, expenditure on solid waste management operation and maintenance was in the order of Rs500 million and increasing by 20% per annum. Most of it is spent from the public health department budget which also funds health centres, promotional campaigns and provision of birth and death certificates. Engineering department budgets covered the cost of vehicle repair and maintenance.

The largest proportion of public health expenditure is on staff costs: this accounted for 84% of the budget between 1991-94. Within this amount, the greatest expenditure is on field staff, including sanitary inspectors, supervisors and sweepers — see Figure 5.

This expenditure has steadily increased due to an annual increase of 11.8% in the total number of field staff employed rather than pay rises to existing staff. Sweepers make up nearly 80% of this staff. Thus most of the budget is spent on recurring costs while capital expenditure remains very low.

This takes place against the backdrop of increasing municipal deficits, suggesting that the current system is not sustainable in the long term; a reduction in the salary bill appears to be a necessary starting point for change.

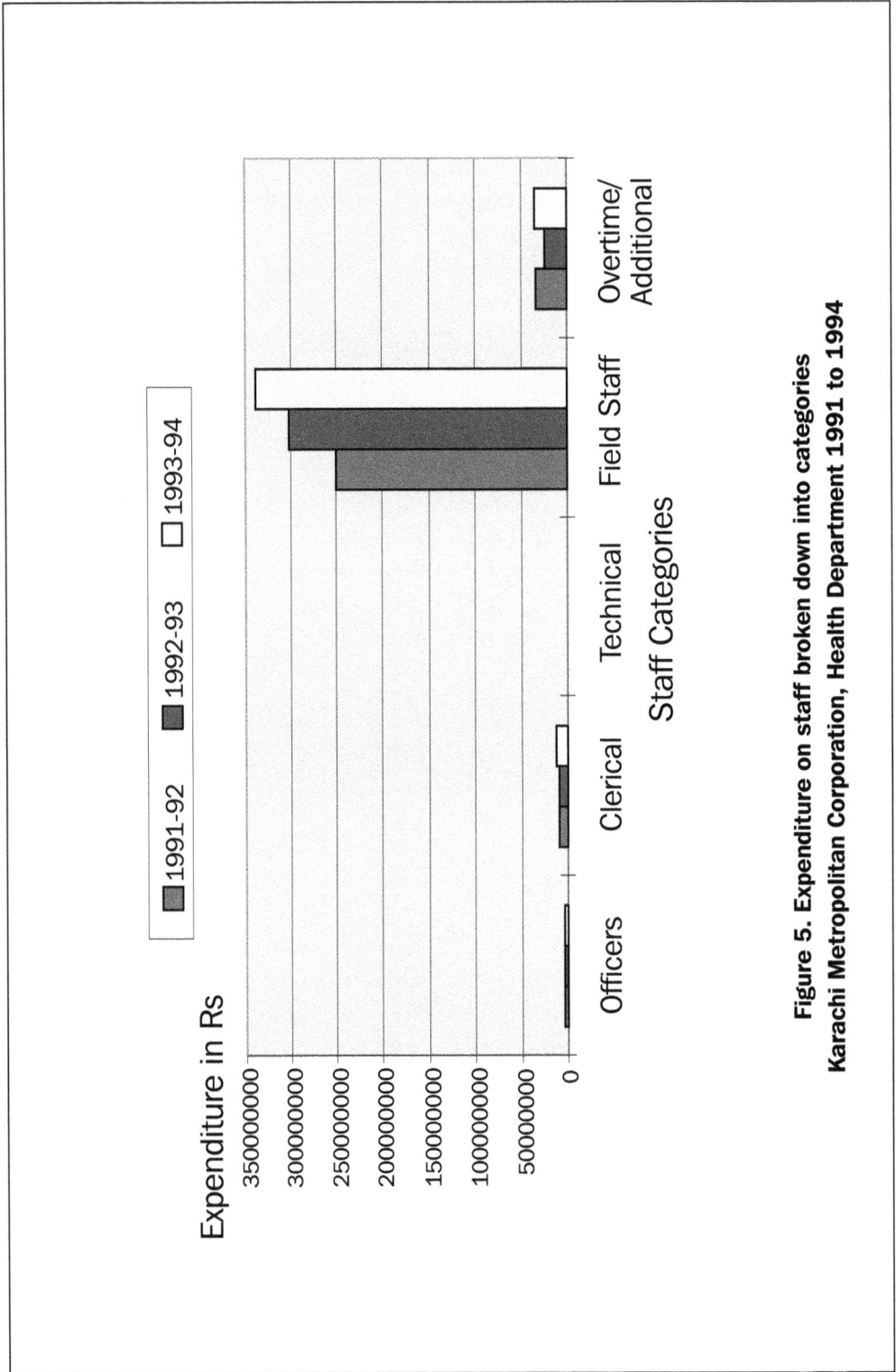

Figure 5. Expenditure on staff broken down into categories
Karachi Metropolitan Corporation, Health Department 1991 to 1994

Staff costs in the health department are unreasonably high, even allowing for the fact that the current solid waste management system is labour-intensive. Any attempt to increase efficiency will inevitably focus on reducing staff numbers. Current revenue streams are insufficient to allow capital investment in safe treatment or disposal systems.

Does the municipality have access to loan or grant assistance? Would it be able to service capital loans?

The previous section showed that it is very unlikely that KMC could fund the additional cost of a landfill operation from ordinary revenue. The little investment that has occurred in recent years was made possible by large grants from aid organisations or loans from international agencies. Such interventions are characterised by strict time frames and possibly inappropriate standards and can have many unforeseen knock-on effects.

KMC would probably be dependent on external support for the funding of a new disposal system. Such support might be available but could result in pressure to achieve unattainable standards. It is advisable to choose the cheapest possible safe system and improve revenue collection, to reduce dependency on outside agencies.

How could recurrent costs be financed?

Based on the previous discussion it is very evident that the recurring cost of waste disposal could be charged directly to the public, at this point. However, KMC could fund the cost through their own budgets.

Even if KMC obtained a loan or grant for capital costs it is not clear how they could cover operation and maintenance costs in the long-term. This will be a major constraint for any system chosen.

Social

Waste picking

What is the extent of waste picking at dump sites? What would be the impact of the proposed options on the livelihood of waste pickers at dump sites? Is there any potential for creating more livelihood opportunities through developing new disposal options?

Waste picking at dumping sites in Karachi is limited to the recovery of metals, since most other re-saleable components are removed earlier in the solid waste management system. The social impact of an improved solid waste system will therefore depend more on changes in collection and transportation. The following scenarios and impacts are anticipated (see Box 14).

Overall, the waste picking at existing disposal sites is not as extensive as waste picking in streets and transfer points, and discussions with waste pickers have revealed that picking is for most of them a part time occupation as they have other opportunities to earn money.

Since there is limited waste picking at disposal sites in Karachi it is not clear what the social effects of a change in disposal practices might be.

Which options maximise access to waste by waste pickers?

Landfilling has the potential to provide access to waste picking as compared with other options such as incineration. Landfilling operation could be designed in such a way that waste picking could be allowed. However, certain hazardous practices such as burning of waste etc. should not be allowed.

Box 14. Improvement scenario and impact on the livelihoods of waste pickers

Scenario	Possible social impact
Improvement in disposal practices without any change in the collection and transportation systems	■ Restricted access to waste pickers. ■ Better environment to surrounding low income areas. ■ Improved environmental health for surrounding residential areas. ■ Income opportunities because of expanded operations at landfill e.g. tea stalls, water etc.
Improvement in the collection, transportation and disposal systems	■ Restricted access to waste pickers. ■ Efficient systems may bring better quality of materials at the disposal end. As a result, waste picking at the disposal end may be an attractive option. ■ Improved environmental health for surrounding residential areas. ■ Income opportunities because of expanded operation at landfill e.g. tea stalls, water etc.
Improvement in the collection and transportation systems with no change in the disposal system	■ More picking at the disposal site. ■ More quantities of waste at the disposal site. ■ Possibly, more burning of waste at the disposal site. ■ Poor environment and health status for surrounding residential areas. ■ Improved environment and health in the city.

Other

What would be the health and income implications for the poor (other than waste pickers)?

Waste disposal sites in Karachi are surrounded by low income areas. Improved practices in waste disposal will result in a significant improvement of the local environment in such areas.

Are the general public aware of the need for better solid waste management?

The general population is not very concerned about the disposal practices and the common view reagrding waste is 'out of sight — out of mind'. However, any disaster or major accident could lead to an increased concern in the public opinion. Recently, a public interest litigation was submitted by a city NGO against the KMC on the installation of a hospital waste incinerator.

Lack of public concern means that it will remain difficult both to control unofficial practices and to generate the willingness to pay for an improved system.

Are there active environmental pressure groups?

There are a number of established NGOs and CBOs in Karachi which are active in promoting a better municipal service and/or indirect service provision. However, they tend to focus on primary collection and secondary storage and to date there has to date been little attention to final disposal. There is certainly no concerted campaign for the establishment of an improved treatment or disposal service.

Another NGO actively promotes composting and recycling but it is very small and again, focuses on activities at household level and the sale of recoverable items to the recycling industry. It has not shown any interest in final disposal.

Since waste disposal is not a priority issue for local NGO's, KMC are unlikely to be subject to lobbying for the adoption of a particular disposal system. Neither, however, can they expect the support and assistance of NGO's in promoting or monitoring or a new service.

Environmental

Initial environmental risks

Are effective environmental health controls in place?

As discussed earlier, there is no regulatory pressure on municipalities to provide an effective solid waste management service. The municipalities in turn have very little control over public waste disposal practices; there is no legislation dealing directly with solid waste management and such indirect legislation as exists (see Table 7) is weak and outdated. Moreover, KMC lack the institutional capacity to enforce it.

Table 7. Legislation related to solid waste management in Pakistan		
Legislation	*Offence*	*Penalty*
Pakistan penal code, 1860 on water pollution	Fouling a public spring or reservoir	Maximum imprisonment of 3 months or fine up to Rs 500
Factories Act 1934 on water pollution	Disposing un-treated industrial waste in water bodies	Fine of Rs 500
Pakistan penal code, 1860 on toxic or hazardous waste	Negligent conduct with respect to poisonous substances	
The Ports Act, 1908 on marine pollution	Discharge of ballast or rubbish into a port	

Generally, regulation and enforcement are not viable tools for improving solid waste management in Pakistan. As a result, there is very little pressure on industry, businesses, institutions or the public to deposit waste at designated sites or in a designated manner.

Lack of municipal control over waste disposal by the public means that any new facilities could be under-utilised, reducing their environmental health benefits. This could also deter the private sector from investing in landfill or other treatment options.

What are the negative impacts of current disposal practices?

The current practice of waste burning to enable the recovery of metal by waste pickers, produces ash which is relatively inert and has little potential to pollute compared with the unburned waste. However, the uncontrolled burning process leads to significant air pollution and associated health and environmental risks. The environmental health hazards arising from current practices are creating a nuisance and warrant investment in safe waste disposal.

Long-term environmental risks

Would the proposed options reduce these negative impacts? Would they lead to long-term environmental improvements?

It is unlikely that significant control could be exerted on the composition of the waste dumped, so site design would be critical for safe and effective waste management.

Design will depend both on the choice of site and on whether waste pickers are allowed to continue burning, which affects the composition of residual waste.

The data in Table 8 is not exhaustive but shows the anticipated risks associated with waste disposal by landfilling in Karachi.

Hazard	Pathway	Receptor	Risk
Table 8. Potential environmental risks associated with waste disposal at Hub River road, Karachi			
Leachate production	Hydrogeological	▪ Groundwater ▪ Potable water supply ▪ People [1] ▪ Watercourses and associated flora and fauna	▪ Pollution of groundwater ▪ Loss of supply ▪ Public health risk ▪ Damage and loss of flora and fauna
Gas migration	▪ Porous soils / geological features ▪ Air via waste	▪ Buildings and other physical structures ▪ People ▪ Air	▪ Explosion / fire ▪ Injury, death, asphyxiation, illness ▪ Global warming, ozone depletion
Exposed clinical waste (sharps, infectious waste)	▪ Direct contact ▪ Purchase of recovered materials	▪ People	▪ Wounding, illness, death
Odour	▪ Air	▪ People	▪ Illness ▪ Public nuisance
Vermin	▪ Waste materials	▪ People	▪ Illness, death
Dust	▪ Air	▪ People	▪ Illness

Further explanation of the risks associated with landfill, and how they can be estimated, is given in Section 5 of this report. It is important to note, however, that in many circumstances a detailed risk analysis is unnecessary and some decisions can be made on the basis of information provided in Table 8 and easily-obtained local data.

Of the options available, landfill stands the best chance of being operated effectively. If this is achieved and unofficial dumping also reduces, environmental hazards from waste disposal should diminish.

The case study of Karachi reveal that landfilling are preferable disposal option for Karachi because of the existing technical, institutional, financial, social and environmental conditions.

Summary

The city of Karachi is currently formulating plans for the development of landfill disposal sites; a situation similar to many cities in low income countries. The city corporation has acquired two sites on the government's land, but their further development needs finances. Providing such finances is beyond the existing capacity of Karachi Metropolitan Corporation (KMC). Such support might be available externally but could result in pressure to achieve unattainable standards. It is advisable to choose the affordable option with the possibility to up-grade it gradually. At the same time, improve revenue collection, to reduce dependency on outside agencies.

The case study clearly demonstrates that considering a number of factors, landfilling appears to be preferable to other disposal options. However, detailed studies should examine the potential for landfill gas and leachate generation to determine the required degree of engineering and pollution control at the detailed design stage. Separate collection of organic waste may facilitate effective composting and may contribute effectively in reducing landfill pollution potential. The relatively low calorific value of waste in Karachi will not support incineration. Waste is also exposed and accessible.

The transportation is irregular in many areas, allowing picking and drying out. The reduction in paper and plastics reduces the combustible component of the waste at the disposal end, making it less suitable for incineration.

The separation of re-saleable items at the household level, during transportation and at final disposal provides livelihoods and valuable additional income for many poor people. Options which remove these opportunities should be avoided. Of all the disposal or treatment options, landfilling provides the greatest opportunity for the utilisation of re-saleable waste.

Municipal capacity to operate and maintain plant and equipment is limited. Of the options available, landfilling may be the most suitable because it employs the simplest technology and systems. Due to a lack of experience within KMC the option chosen should first be piloted at one site, to develop expertise which can be used for training other staff and eventual expansion. The planning and design of any future waste disposal operation will have to include careful human resource planning as many of the skills required are not locally available at present. Options requiring advanced and rare technical skills should be avoided, making landfilling the most viable option.

Karachi Metropolitan Corporation are under no immediate pressure to enforce current laws and ordinances to improve waste disposal practice. This could lead to complacency in operating any new system and strengthens the case for the simplest possible disposal option.

Lack of political commitment could threaten the long-term operation and monitoring of any waste treatment/disposal system. Options with high running costs would be particularly vulnerable to changes in municipal priorities. Disposal options need reliable operation and maintenance systems as they are central to the other stages. This needs a strong and sustainable political commitment.

The standards and safety of a landfill site in Karachi depends upon the risk taking capacity of the population and the environment. Reducing the potential risks means increasing the cost. The standards to be adopted must be a compromise between affordable risks and cost. This could lead to the technology to be adopted. The next section reviews the available landfill guidelines in a risk assessment framework.

Section 5

Principles and Practices for
Appropriate Landfill: A Review

Introduction

The disposal of solid waste to land has been widespread ever since population growth and industrialisation made it necessary to pay special attention to waste management. In many low income countries, this need arose quite recently.

Since disposal to land can vary from simple dumping to highly engineered landfill, it accommodates a wide range of disposal needs and budgets in a way that incineration and other capital intensive options cannot. This flexibility, coupled with risk control through appropriate design and management, will ensure that landfill remains an important waste management option in low income countries. Even if other options are used, there will always be a proportion of the waste stream that needs disposal. In the past, little attention was paid to developing appropriate landfill guidelines for low income countries. Most guidance was based on highly engineered techniques used in the high income countries and was not always appropriate to countries where scarce funds had to be reserved for issues that affected communities more directly.

This review presents information that will aid decision-making processes in relation to appropriate landfill planning, engineering and operation and should be viewed within the risk assessment framework.

According to Ball and Legg (1997), 'The objective of appropriate technology for landfilling in low income countries countries is to match the desired protection of public health and environment, afforded by modern landfill theory, with the realities of ambient environmental standards and affordability, existing in developing countries'. In many low income countries, open dumping remains the most common disposal method, and according to Rushbrook and Finnecy (1988) these unacceptable waste disposal facilities, often sited immediately adjacent to residential areas, generally contravene all the accepted landfill principles, with regard to siting, design and operation.

However, the importance of waste management goes beyond environmental and healthcare issues. According to Schubeler (1996), 'With its broad implications and close links to other sectors, municipal solid waste management constitutes an important entry point for integrated urban management support'.

Box 15. Goals for municipal solid waste management

Four goals of municipal solid waste management (Schubeler, 1996)

1. Protection of environmental health.

2. Promotion of the quality of the urban environment.

3. Supporting the efficiency and productivity of the economy.

4. Generation of employment and income.

The importance of socio-economic considerations in the identification of sustainable waste management options is clearly identified through these goals. According to Schubeler (1996), 'The essential condition of sustainability implies that waste management systems must be *absorbed and carried by the society* and its local communities. These systems must, in other words, be *appropriate* to the particular circumstances and problems of the city and the locality, employing and developing the capacities of all stakeholders, including the households and communities requiring service, private sector enterprises and workers (both formal and informal), and government agencies at the local, regional and national levels'.

When circumstances change and the community becomes more affluent, then it may be possible to modify waste management policy and practice in the light of these changes. Schubeler has suggested an upgrade 'pathway' for landfill sites from open dumping to sanitary landfill via controlled dumping and engineered landfill and with appropriate consideration of local conditions could provide for planned upgrade as the necessary finance becomes available.

Thus, the most appropriate landfill systems for developing countries will be those which make an effective compromise between environmental protection and cost. That is not to say, however, that countries should accept open dumping on the basis that 'we cannot afford anything else'. The World Health Organisation (WHO, 1995) have recommended that all local authorities should identify suitable sites for landfill in their long-term plans and that these sites should be operated to a standard that protects human health and the environment.

This section looks at principles of landfill design and operation, including the new concept of sustainable landfill. This has emerged in response to the growing recognition of the need to account for long-term as well as short-term pollution potential. Some key, fundamental information on landfill gas and leachate is also presented and this can be used to inform landfill decision-making processes.

A simple liner to control leachate and gas migration costs approximately US$25/m² (in 1999). Leachate accumulating on the liner requires treatment at a cost of approximately US$20/m³. In affluent countries where daily exposure to risks is low such costs are both affordable and justifiable. In poorer countries, however, many immediate risks are present (such as disease, malnutrition etc.) and warrant higher priority.

There are a number of large, detailed texts relating to landfill design and control that against a background of relatively little knowledge can provide too much information to assimilate. The purpose of this section is to provide an overview of current principles and practice in landfill design and management so that practitioners can develop a clear view of why it is important to control landfill-associated risks. The overview of principles will facilitate identification of the design and management system most likely to succeed within a local context, while the brief overview of the two main hazards (landfill gas and leachate) will direct detailed design considerations. With a clearer understanding of the above, the reader may then more usefully use these other texts that have already addressed landfill design in low income countries in great detail (See bibliography).

This section is written within a risk management framework and commences with an introduction before addressing the main landfill design principles. The concept of risk assessment is then introduced before looking at risk control mechanisms including options other than design options (e.g. control through operational planning). The final part provides fundamental information relating to landfill gas and leachate so that with this understanding, control mechanisms can be modified to suit local needs.

When undertaking risk assessments it is important to set them in the context of the risks to which a community is exposed every day. There is little to gain from setting unrealistic targets and it may be more helpful to think in terms of upgrading step-by-step, as finance and capacity allows, from open dumping to sanitary landfill via controlled dumping and engineered landfill (Rushbrook and Pugh, 1998).

Principles of landfill

The term landfill commonly refers to the *engineered* deposit of waste onto and into land (ISWA, 1992). However, it may not be necessary to use an engineered site where the waste is largely inert at final disposal, for example, in rural villages where it contains a large proportion of soil and dirt from sweeping. In such cases, non-engineered disposal on designated land can be a simple, sustainable and successful means of waste management.

In the light of the above, the following definition is applicable in developing countries:

'Landfill is the deposit of waste onto and into land in such a way that the environmental risk is controlled at an appropriate and acceptable level and where, subsequent to disposal, the land can made available for other uses'.

Rushbrook and Pugh (1998) have also defined a sanitary landfill as one which involves 'the continuing refinement and increasing complexity in the engineering design and construction techniques begun in the engineered landfill stage. In addition, engineered landfills are more likely to have the pre-planned installation of landfill gas control or utilisation measures, extensive environmental monitoring, a highly organised and trained work force, detailed record keeping by the site office staff, and, where circumstances dictate, on-site treatment to supplement a leachate collection system'. The attainment of these standards will not be achieved in many countries in the foreseeable future and therefore for many, more appropriate standards should apply.

Four minimum requirements for a sanitary landfill (Rushbrook and Pugh, 1998):

■ Full or partial hydrogeological isolation.

■ Formal engineering preparations.

■ Permanent control.

■ Planned waste emplacement and covering.

In relation to waste disposal in sub-Saharan Africa, Ball (1998) concluded that:

■ Appropriate technology must be affordable and sustainable in the long-term.

■ Guidelines should ensure appropriate technology and sustainable operations for both large and small communities.

■ Strategies were needed to prevent dumping of hazardous waste at landfills, especially where pickers are present.

Box 16. Ten principles applicable to African waste disposal projects (Ball, 1998)

Focus on the local situation

1. Spend maximum time locally to ensure a good sound knowledge of the situation.
2. Build on the local situation, taking cognisance of existing disposal sites and politics.
3. Improve generally on the *Status Quo,* as opposed to attempting the limited ideal.

Ensure appropriate standards

4. Ensure consistent standards, with regard to other waste management components.
5. Where necessary, adapt standards defensibly, ensuring sound scientific reasoning.
6. Avoid 'imported' industrialised country standards, which are seldom appropriate.

Ensure long-term sustainability

7. Properly remediate and close existing dumps, before abandoning them.
8. Progressively upgrade facilities, possibly remediating them through operation.
9. Build capacity by training. Leave someone behind who is capable and responsible.
10. Ensure ongoing involvement, by means of audits and other control measures.

While the above were formulated with respect to Africa, they are equally as applicable in other low and middle income countries.

Based on experience from Africa, Ball et al (1993, 1995, 1996) have advocated a sustainable system where minimum design requirements are based on a landfill classification which uses three criteria for assessment. These are the waste type, the size of the landfill operation, and the potential for leachate generation. Using this system, proposed standards are more relaxed for general waste, low-volume waste streams and for low potential for leachate generation.

Within this classification system, the waste type can either be general waste or hazardous waste. The size of the landfill operation is divided into four categories (Table 9) and is based on the maximum rate of deposition per day.

Table 9. Criteria for the size class of landfill	
Size class	*Maximum rate of deposition (tonnes per day)*
Communal	Up to 1
Small	Between 1 and 25
Medium	Between 25 and 500
Large	More than 500

The potential for leachate generation is assessed as either being significant or sporadic and is calculated using a simplified site water balance calculation.

Using these criteria, and data collected in support of the assessment, the minimum requirements for a range of factors are determined. These include cut-off drainage systems, separation between the waste body and groundwater, underliner systems, leachate and contaminated water collection systems, provision of adequate covering, slope stability, security, infrastructure, end-use and gas control. This system has been applied successfully in South Africa and elsewhere in Southern Africa and provides an example of a systematic approach to the design of appropriate facilities that account for local conditions and which can lead to the identification of more affordable solutions to the waste disposal problem. It does not account for socio-economic or political considerations *per se*, but the assessment procedure follows the landfill development sequence where such issues could be considered during the site selection process.

This system provides a methodology for reaching an engineering compromise between environmental protection and cost, described above. However, in the current work we have also looked at other means than engineering to help to control landfill-related environmental risks.

Landfill design principles
Where the waste deposited is not totally inert, landfill design principles have been developed primarily to deal with leachate management. The key design principles are explained below.

Dilute and attenuate

This is the guiding principle of landfill disposal in unconfined sites with little or no engineering of the site boundary. It allows leachate to migrate to the surrounding environment and relies upon attenuation both within the waste and in the surrounding geology, by biological and physico-chemical processes. Dilution within groundwater further reduces the risk posed by the leachate but by definition *also* contaminates the groundwater.

This principle is only applicable where a risk assessment (see later) indicates that the risk posed by the leachate will be acceptable. In very rare cases where attenuation will not take place in the environment then a process of *dilute and disperse* will prevail.

Where the leachate is hazardous, attenuation cannot be relied upon in all circumstances and containment may be more appropriate (see below).

Containment

It is based on the principle that leachate should not be allowed to migrate beyond the site boundary. Instead, it accumulates and has to be treated (see entombment). Depending on site engineering, gas migration may also be controlled. Containment requires a much greater degree of site design, engineering, and management but enables tighter hazard control.

Due to the complex and expensive techniques involved in containment landfill it is not always viable in low income countries. However, where the waste is clearly hazardous, containment is essential and can sometimes be achieved using a natural clay barrier.

Entombment (Dry-tomb)

This approach prevents liquid infiltration so that the waste remains dry. If the emplaced waste is dry then it will not decompose, and will not produce a polluting leachate. It is not suitable for organic waste but can be simple, cheap and effective for the disposal of inert wastes.

Dry-tomb landfill is, however, an extreme form of pollution control and will be unsustainable for many waste streams because it is a form of storage rather than treatment. When used for non-inert wastes it will ultimately cause pollution when environmental conditions change and containment fails. This could happen, for example, when an area of previously low rainfall experiences climate change.

Moreover, entombment cannot prevent the formation or release of leachate altogether. There will always be some risk of pollution which could be very serious where materials with high pollution potential such as municipal solid waste were present.

In short, the 'dry-tomb' approach transfers waste management problems to future generations. It is not an appropriate way forward for landfill management, except in rare situations where a risk assessment indicates otherwise or for inert wastes.

Flushing bioreactor

This uses enhanced biological degradation to reduce the organic content of waste (and hence its hazardous nature) and liquid flushing to remove waste products including ammonia and other relatively non-degradable compounds. It thereby aims to produce a 'stable waste' within 30 years of emplacement and so ensure that the risk to the environment will be at an acceptable level when liner failure occurs.

This design concept has been developed for waste management in high income countries and due to its cost may not be appropriate in low income countries. Furthermore, there has so far been little practical experience with flushing bioreactors.

Landraising

Landraising can operate according to any of the above principles and involves the emplacement of waste above ground. This may not reduce the hazards arising but, if constructed with a base at ground level, greatly facilitates control of gas and leachate. The method is attracting increasing interest as it can augment the protection afforded by other options described above.

Landraising has several potential advantages and with a supporting risk assessment it can:

■ Enable the use of otherwise unsuitable sites (e.g. where there is an underlying aquifer).

■ Enable the use of clay sites without a complementary liner (see later).

■ Allow more waste to be deposited for a given area (subject to planning considerations), reducing costs.

It could, therefore, be useful in many locations in low income countries.

These design principles apply upon selection of a particular site and the detailed engineering will vary according to local factors such as the local geology/hydrogeology, the availability of engineering materials and the proximity/location of sensitive receptors.

Sustainable landfill

The ten principles described by Ball (Box 15) could be summarised by the term 'sustainable landfill'. This term relates to the objectives of landfilling rather than a specific design or operation. It has been defined by Westlake (1997) as

'a landfill designed and operated in such a way that minimises both short-term and long-term environmental risks to an acceptable level'.

The vision of sustainable landfill is that each generation should manage its waste so that within 30 years it reaches final disposal quality, i.e. 'the stage when any emissions to the environment are acceptable without further treatment' (Harris *et al*, 1993). Whichever of the above design principles is adopted, sustainable landfilling should be the ultimate objective and for many low income countries is achievable through the ten principles (Box 15) that have been identified by Ball (1998). These will be modified and supplemented by locally-determined factors to ensure that any risks that may arise, now or in the future, are acceptable.

Fail-safe landfill

This concept is related to sustainable landfill and works on the assumption that any containment system will ultimately fail and/or institutional control will cease, releasing gas and leachate (Loxham, 1993). Any releases should therefore pose no unacceptable risk to the environment, and this requires pre-treatment or accelerated degradation of the waste.

Fail-safe design involves four steps:

1. Analysis of how the engineering will fail.

2. Definition of the sort of environment in which the failure will occur.

3. Assessment of the environmental impact of failure.

4. Estimation of the probability of failure.

Following this approach, the landfill may be designed in such a way that when failure occurs, the environmental risks will be at an acceptable level.

Risk assessment and appropriate landfill

Risk assessment should be integral to the design process in order to develop a cost-efficient operation that responds to local environmental conditions.

The hazards associated with landfill vary according to:

- The nature of the waste.

- Conditions within the landfill.

- The nature of the surrounding environment.

A **hazard** is any event which has the potential to be harmful. When a pathway is present by which a sensitive receptor (target) can be harmed by that event, then there is an associated **risk**.

If a risk is present, it will be possible to demonstrate a pollution linkage whereby a sensitive receptor is subject to a hazardous event via a pollution pathway:

HAZARD ———— PATHWAY ———— RECEPTOR

For there to be a risk, **ALL THREE** factors must be present. It follows that a risk can be prevented through controlling either the hazard, the pathway or the receptor. Landfill engineering essentially addresses the pathway element, but in many cases it may be easier to reduce the hazard term through waste input control (e.g. by removing organic waste for composting).

For example, in the above pollution linkage, the hazard may be landfill leachate generated from a mixture of inert and organic waste, which migrates via groundwater (the pathway) to harm drinking water and humans (the sensitive receptor in this example). If there is no hazard (because, in this example, all degradable waste has been removed for composting) there will be no risk to humans. If there are no sensitive receptors (humans), then nothing can be harmed (in this particular pollution linkage) and there will be no risk. Finally, if there is no pathway (in this case groundwater) then there is nothing that will allow the hazard to reach the sensitive receptor.

Thinking of landfill control in this way can allow a number of different options for risk control to be considered and the most appropriate solution identified.

The risk assessment process comprises four stages of investigation (terms in parentheses are those commonly used in the USA):

1. **Hazard identification** (indicator chemical selection). This may include determination of leachate composition.

2. **Hazard analysis** (exposure assessment). The process of determining releases or event probabilities. This could include determination of the routes via which leachate could reach sensitive receptors (e.g. people, groundwater), and the characteristics of these receptors.

3. **Risk estimation** (toxicity assessment). The process of assessing potential harm by determining the dose-effect relationship between pollutant and receptor.

4. **Risk evaluation** (risk characterisation). Assessment of whether the estimated level of risk is acceptable.

(Petts, 1993)

In practice there can be serious difficulties in carrying out an accurate risk assessment because:

- Baseline data may be incomplete and there are many uncertainties, for example, the manner in which leachate passes through geological strata.
- The cost of a quantitative risk assessment can be very high.

However, in many cases a qualitative judgment may be sufficient; the real value of the framework is that it provides a structured approach to studying the relationship between cause and effect (Petts, 1993). In many circumstances, it may not be necessary to go beyond the hazard analysis stage. Thus, for an isolated landfill site where the hazard element is low (e.g. little or no leachate and gas production) it will be difficult to justify the use of expensive landfill lining systems or leachate treatment plant (which in any case may not be feasible because of the uncertainty of electricity supply). However, it may be possible to justify designing a small landraise scheme in which easily under-taken ground engineering is used to prepare a relatively impermeable base to the site, and where any weak leachate which is generated is allowed to flow under gravity through a cheaply constructed plant root treatment system before discharge to surface watercourse In this case, a risk assessment approach can support appropriate and affordable control by controlling the pathway element in a way which more prescriptive controls could not.

Landfill risk control mechanisms

Engineering options to control landfill gas and leachate are discussed in the following sections. In addition, some other potential controls include the following.

Control through operational planning

Many landfill-associated risks can be controlled or avoided through effective planning. Some examples of planning interventions for risk control are given below.

Control of waste inputs

For effective landfill management it is important to appreciate the characteristics of the waste deposited and its harmful potential. Care is needed here, since many household wastes can be more damaging to the environment than some classified as hazardous.

Box 17. The main types of waste

Waste components are mostly classified according to their source rather than their specific nature. Common types and definitions are as follows:

- *Inert waste* comprises material which will not give rise to harmful chemical or biological agents when placed in landfill.

- *Household waste* is waste generated in private homes.

- *Municipal waste* comprises household waste and other wastes collected by local authorities including road sweepings and parks and gardens waste; both can contain hazardous materials but present the highest environmental risk through their potential to produce a high BOD leachate and landfill gas.

- *Commercial waste* is collected from commercial premises, but is not necessarily any less hazardous than industrial waste collected from industrial premises (e.g. large amounts of paper and card waste can degrade within a landfill to produce landfill gas and leachate).

- *Hazardous waste* is normally used to describe waste that is hazardous irrespective of its origins; detailed definitions vary considerably.

- *Healthcare waste*, also known as *clinical* or *medical* waste contains anything from flowers to infectious agents, and risks can vary accordingly.

Furthermore, waste of one category often contains some of other types unless there is meticulous (and expensive) input control. It is not unusual for so-called inert landfill sites to produce large amounts of methane gas because of contamination with materials which are not actually inert.

If the waste needing disposal is inert the associated hazards will be minimal and simple treatment or disposal options may become possible. There is therefore much to gain from promoting waste separation and recycling (by householders and the informal sector) and restricting the deposit of highly hazardous material. While this may be difficult from a social or political perspective, it may obviate the need for expensive landfill control mechanisms.

Disposal of healthcare waste

In many low income countries healthcare wastes are disposed at landfill together with other general wastes and can lead to injury and illness amongst waste pickers. Separation from other municipal waste can therefore be an effective and affordable way of controlling the associated risks.

Destruction of healthcare waste by highly-controlled incineration is expensive, but an alternative is to emplace it in a specially-designated and controlled area of the landfill site where access is restricted. The waste must be covered immediately after emplacement as it may have value on the open market. In Addis Ababa, for example, serum (drip) bags are recovered, made into handbags and sold.

In the examples above, control of waste inputs, either through separation on site or through segregation to control waste arriving for disposal (e.g. through diversion to composting of organic waste) can help to control environmental risks in a cost-effective manner. This is not a simple procedure and may carry socio-economic, political and infrastructural considerations, it is likely to provide long-term and more sustainable solutions.

Access restrictions

Since it is not always possible to separate hazardous waste from more inert components it is important to control public access to landfill sites. This is not easily done, however, as there are often dozens or even hundreds of waste pickers working at disposal sites in organised gangs. Excluding people who make their living from waste is also politically controversial and would require strong political support if it were to go ahead. An assessment of the social consequences must be undertaken before a decision to exclude waste pickers from the disposal site is considered.

> It is probably a more realistic aim to reduce the amount of hazardous waste to which pickers are exposed than to exclude them from sites altogether. In this case, risk control is effected by controlling the hazard term in the pollution linkage, rather than removing the sensitive receptor. It may be less effective in controlling human health risks, but will be achievable in a way that removing pickers may not (and in which case there would be no risk reduction).

Site location

Too often, municipal authorities choose a site on the basis of cost, land ownership or road access without due regard to other factors (such as geology) which affect risks significantly. While political and social issues should be acknowledged in the site selection procedure, Ball and Legg (1997) have identified that it is imperative that the choice of site is based on technical merits and not the whims of politicians, for if a site is chosen for purely political expedience, it is likely to prove problematic at a later stage.

Operational controls

Risk control can also be effected through operational controls such as surface water management, nuisance control (e.g litter, odour) and occupational health and safety. Operational control of site engineering which will be required in the form of earthworks, for example, grading the base or sides of the site, formation or embankments; removal of overburden; earth bank construction on perimeter; access roads; cell construction and waste compaction - all requiring appropriate equipment and safety procedures.

The engineering of landfill sites for lining is a technically complex measure and is addressed in more detail in a following section.

In order to reduce the potential risks associated with leachate production, any ingress of ground or surface water must be diverted away to minimise leachate production. Surface water preparatory work may include a peripheral ditch system; sealing barriers for water course adjacent to the site; soakaways; weirs, bunds, even small dams. Groundwater engineering may include excavation to the impervious strata and backfilling with drainage and/or sealing materials. Leachate collection sumps for collection, and tanks or lagoons for treatment together with pipework and pump systems, weirs and pen-stocks are examples of engineering for leachate risk management, which through effective operational controls will help to ensure acceptable risk to the environment. Nuisance control can also be very important, particularly if the site is near housing or areas used by the public.

Litter can be controlled by:

- Depositing wastes at the base of face at a lower level than the rest of the site.

- Litter fencing along bund walls.

- Mobile litter screens **close** to the working area and regularly cleaned
- Covered vehicles with waste compacted into face as soon as possible after arrival of vehicle.

- Damping of some wastes in dry weather.

Objectionable odours will be reduced by good site management. Odour is likely to be a nuisance rather than a heatlh hazard provided that there is sufficient dilution of land gas to keep methane concentrations below the Lower Explosive Limit (5% in air).

The principal ways of minimising odours are:

- Good compaction and suitable gradients and adequate cover to minimise water ingress.
- Immediate deposition of delivered waste.
- Waste should not be deposited in standing water.
- Other stronger and ameliorative action may include.
- Improving drainage.
- Spreading hydrated lime over newly saturated waste.
- Flaring landfill gas.
- Increasing cover thickness.

Site workers and waste pickers are generally more vulnerable to the poor health and safety standards at the landfill sites. Many hazards of landfills are of course common to other workplaces, however, some of the more specific health hazards on landfill sites are:

- Consignors failing to declare the true and precise nature of a waste.
- Hazards resulting from the mixing of incompatible wastes.
- The hazards of specific wastes e.g. asbestos.
- The hazards of all weather working e.g. handling dusty wastes in dry windy conditions, or solvent bearing wastes in hot still weather.

Monitoring is an essential part of landfill operations both during the life of the site and also throughout the aftercare period.

Control through design

An important principle in landfill design is to 'keep it simple' since complex features stand a greater chance of failure (Rushbrook and Pugh, 1998). Furthermore, Rushbrook and Pugh (1998) have said that 'the higher the level of complexity of the intervention, the greater the risk of its failure', and that 'priority should, therefore, be given to measures to overcome areas of concern which offer the lowest risk of failure, and that the principle of 'keep it simple' should be considered at all stages of development'. Ball (1998) has also said that appropriate standards are usually sustainable, whereas imported standards are usually not.

Landraising is a good example of simple, effective design as discussed. This in conjunction with organic composting may be an affordable way to reduce risks to an acceptable level without resorting to expensive engineering controls, especially if the site has been well-selected.

In developing countries, effective engineering must take account of environmental risks and financial constraints and must provide appropriate control that may be quite different from that elsewhere in the world. Engineering controls that can be used should circumstances allow, are discussed in more details in the following sections.

Control through aftercare

Landfill aftercare includes maintenance of the restored site and any activities necessary to control pollution. In some cases organic waste has the potential to pollute for many hundreds of years.

Upon completion of the active phase of landfill, the site must be restored in such a way that is appropriate to the surroundings, that minimises the risk to the environment, and which preferably has potential to support productive land-use. Landfill restoration is not a 'one-off' process, but one that requires monitoring and control for as long as there is an associated risk to the environment.

> The nature and extent of the risk will be determined by factors such as the type of waste, historical operating procedures, site geology and hydrogeology, and the location and sensitivity of receptors that may be affected by the potential emissions from the restored landfill.

Effective landfill restoration requires that the restoration planning is conducted at the design stage, so that site development, materials (engineering materials, daily cover etc.) movement and purchase, costing, etc. can all be undertaken, thus ensuring that the landfill development occurs in the most efficient manner, and which accounts for the many costs associated with this stage of landfill development.

The intended end-use of the site will obviously make a big difference, and will be constrained by a number of factors including:

- The physical nature of the waste (e.g. affecting load-bearing capacity, potential for combustion/corrosion etc.).
- Anticipated settling.
- The level of gaseous emissions.
- The nature of the surrounding land and land uses.
- Local topography.
- Materials availability (affecting, for example, the type of available top-soil, and the activities which it will support).

Aftercare requirements include the maintenance of the restored landfill, and any activities necessary to deal with the potential for environmental pollution. This potential may remain for many hundreds of years according to a number of factors including the nature of the emplaced waste, and the management of the landfill. In a truly sustainable landfill, the aftercare period should relatively small, and so the long-term costs and liabilities would be correspondingly short. Financial factors such as these will be equally as important as legislation in encouraging more sustainable waste management. In more rural areas within developing countries, the wastes are often relatively inert, and in these cases, little may be required with respect to aftercare provisions and there will be little in the way of significant environmental liabilities.

According to the chosen site afteruse, aftercare tasks may include:

- monitoring of landfill gas and leachate

- monitoring of the surrounding environment (eg groundwater)

- landfill cap maintenance, e.g. grading to counter differential settlement

- crop (eg trees, pasture) management for effective production and maintenance of cap integrity.

Where there is more significant potential to pollute, UNEP (1994) have identified the main aspects to be monitored as:

- erosion control (including maintenance of surface drainage systems)

- observation of settlement and possible deformations

- groundwater monitoring

- leachate and gas control

- meteorological data

- observation of the condition of vegetation and presence of vermin and odours.

Landfill gas and leachate

Under most circumstances, landfill gas and leachate comprise the major hazards associated with landfill. They are produced by bacteriological degradation of waste, which occurs under anaerobic conditions.

Box 18. Breakdown of the biodegradable material within municipal waste

Within waste disposed to landfill, any organic matter including vegetable matter, paper and cardboard and to some extent, textiles are biodegradable. The composition of municipal waste varies from country to country and will vary from season to season and thus the potential to pollute will vary accordingly. Carbohydrates comprise a large percentage of the **biodegradable** material within municipal refuse, the overall breakdown of which can be represented by the equation:

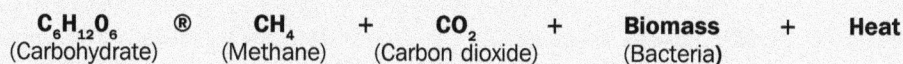

$$C_6H_{12}O_6 \quad ® \quad CH_4 \quad + \quad CO_2 \quad + \quad Biomass \quad + \quad Heat$$

(Carbohydrate)   (Methane)   (Carbon dioxide)   (Bacteria)

Landfill leachate may contaminate the surrounding land and water, including drinking water, while landfill gas which can be toxic, can lead to global warming and has been responsible for a number of explosions leading to human fatalities.

It is not possible to contain waste or its products within landfill for ever, and once pollutants are released, we cannot guarantee that sensitive receptors will not be affected. Hazard control is, therefore, the most effective tool for reducing the overall risk associated with landfill. It can also be cost-effective in low income countries as it may obviate the need for expensive engineering controls.

The deposition of waste containing biodegradable matter invariably leads to the production of gas and leachate, the composition of which depends on many factors, including:

- The nature of the waste.
- Moisture content.
- pH.
- Waste particle size and density.
- Temperature.

Moisture content

Most micro-organisms including bacteria require a minimum of approximately 12% (by weight) moisture for growth, and thus the moisture content of landfilled waste will be an important factor in determining the amount and extent of gas and leachate production. In fact, for biodegradable waste, moisture content is probably the single most important factor affecting gas production in landfill.

pH

The activity of all micro-organisms is affected by pH, and the methanogenic bacteria within landfill which produce methane gas will only grow within a narrow pH range around neutrality. In terms of leachate composition, landfill development is often described as being in the acetogenic leachate phase (acid generating) or the methanogenic leachate phase (methane generating). The stage of development is determined simply by measuring the pH, and can provide useful information for overall landfill management. The switch from acetogenic to methanogenic phase can occur very quickly, a factor which is difficult to explain, and which if understood, could facilitate more effective control of waste degradation processes generally.

Waste particle size and density

The size of waste particles will affect the density that can be achieved upon compaction and will also affect the surface area : volume ratio. Each will affect moisture absorption and potential for biological degradation, although in the context of landfill, neither is fully understood.

Temperature

Microbial activity is affected by temperature to the extent that we are able to segregate bacteria according to their optimum temperature operating conditions. Thus, factors affecting landfill temperatures are likely to affect microbial activity and hence gas production. An increase in temperature tends to increase gas production.

Landfill gas

Production

The nature of the hazard caused by landfill gas and any potential benefits (e.g. from electricity generation) will depend on its specific composition as well as local environmental conditions.

Box 19. Landfill gas yield

The amount of gas produced by landfilled waste varies according to local conditions but a theoretical yield can be predicted using the Buswell equation (Buswell and Hatfield, 1939). This requires knowledge of the elemental composition of a waste and assumes it is 100% degradable. The original Buswell equation which has since been extended and made more complex is as follows:

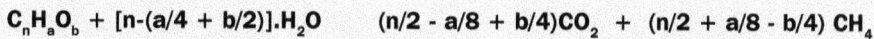

$$C_nH_aO_b + [n-(a/4 + b/2)].H_2O \quad (n/2 - a/8 + b/4)CO_2 + (n/2 + a/8 - b/4) CH_4$$

Where C, H and O represent carbon, hydrogen and oxygen respectively and n, a, and b represent the number of molecules of each.

Other methods for calculating gas yields are summarised in a report of Biostrategy Associates Ltd on behalf of ETSU (1992).

Composition and properties

Typical landfill gas contains a number of components which tend to occur within a characteristic range and so provide a means of distinguishing landfill from other gases.

Box 20. Landfill gas composition

Once waste has become methanogenic (has commenced producing methane gas), landfill gas contains mostly:

- *Methane,* a colourless, odourless, flammable gas, with a density lighter than air. It typically makes up 50-60% of landfill gas (v/v).

- *Carbon dioxide,* also colourless and odourless, but non-flammable and denser than air. This typically accounts for 30-40% (v/v).

Other 'bulk' components of landfill gas can include:

- *Hydrogen (especially in the early stages of degradation).*

- *Oxygen.* The flammability of methane depends on the presence of oxygen, so it is important to control oxygen levels where gas abstraction is undertaken. The level of oxygen within the system is commonly used to monitor abstraction rates and control the rate of gas pumping.

- *Nitrogen.* This is essentially inert and will have little affect except to modify the explosive range for methane which varies according to the gas mixture in which the methane is found.

When present, the latter two gases normally indicate air ingress within the landfill.

Risks arising from landfill gas

Explosion and fire

Both methane and hydrogen are flammable in the presence of oxygen and potentially explosive in a confined environment. Methane is flammable in air within the range 5-15% by volume, while hydrogen is flammable within the range 4.1-7.5%. However, hydrogen is seldom present at levels within the explosive range.

Methane is often present within waste at levels above 15%. However, dilution during migration causes concentrations to fall to within the flammable range and there have been many examples around the world of landfill gas-associated incidents involving explosions, fires, human death and injury (Gendebien et al,1992).

Where the escaping gas is not confined, the explosion risk is lower but there is a risk of fire. With good landfill site management the potential for fires decreases, but in the past many landfill operators accepted that minor fires were an inevitable part of the operation. When fires occur within the waste itself, they can be extremely difficult to extinguish and can lead to uncontrolled and unpredictable subsidence, and the production of smoke and toxic fumes. In many cases, the only way of extinguishing such fires is to remove the waste, and dig out the flammable material to the surface where it can be dealt with more easily. This process, in itself, is extremely hazardous.

Oxygen deprivation of plant roots due to gas migration may also occur, leading to vegetation 'die-back'. Where gas migration has occurred, the pathway is often indicated by surface vegetation, including trees, which show withering at leaf margins, defoliation, and branch die-back.

Trace components

The trace components of landfill gas comprise mostly alkanes and alkenes, and their oxidation products (aldehydes, ketones, alcohols and esters). Many of them are recognised toxicants when present in air at concentrations above established toxicity threshold limit values (TLVs) or Occupational Exposure Standards. However, in most workplaces significant dilution occurs through mixing with air, reducing levels to below standard limits. It is, nevertheless, important to recognise the hazards and potentially dangerous situations.

Global warming

Global warming (also known as the greenhouse effect) is the warming of the Earth's atmosphere by the accumulation of gases that absorb reflected solar radiation. These gases include methane, carbon dioxide, and chlorofluoro-carbons. The potential long-term consequences of global warming include climate change, sea level rises (as a result of melting of polar ice), desertification, and changing food production.

There has been a steady increase in atmospheric methane in recent years (Blake and Rowland, 1988). Globally, landfill contributes 8-20% of total anthropogenic (man-made) emissions (IPCC, 1992).

Landfill gas migration

During landfill development most gas produced will vent to the atmosphere provided permeable intermediate cover has been used. After final capping, venting will be restricted causing gas pressure to develop within the landfill and may lead to lateral migration.

Gas migration is affected essentially by physical factors. Biological and chemical processes are more significant in affecting gas composition, through processes such as methane oxidation which converts methane to carbon dioxide.

Relevant physical factors include:

- **Environmental** conditions within the waste. These affect the rate of degradation and gas pressure build up.

- **Geophysical** conditions. These affect migration pathways. Where there is a route such as fractured geological strata or a mine shaft, the gas may travel large distances unless restricted by the water table. In varied lithologies, it tends to migrate preferentially through the most permeable rock as well as through caves and other pathways of least resistance.

- **Climatic** conditions, including:
  - Falling atmospheric pressure. This causes the surface pressures opposing gas migration to decrease, so facilitating gas movement from the landfill.
  - Rainfall. This makes surface material swell and close cracks, reducing vertical migration pathways and increasing the potential for lateral migration.
  - Water infiltration. This can also raise the water table and leachate levels within the site, reducing gas volume and increasing gas pressure.

The variability of gas emissions is determined by the proportion of void space in the ground, rather than permeability.

Control of landfill gas

Given the dangers associated with landfill gas, effective control of emissions is important and can be effected by:

- Controlling waste inputs (to restrict the amount of organic waste) or

- Controlling processes within the waste (e.g. minimising moisture content to limit gas production),

- Controlling the migration process (via physical barriers, or vents to remove gas from the site and reduce gas pressure).

Physical barriers are of limited use in preventing migration; even if they are impermeable they simply re-direct the gas to vent in another direction, e.g. vertically.

Since gas migration cannot easily be prevented, removal is often the preferred option. This is done using:

- 'within waste vents' (wells) through which the gas can be extracted either actively or passively, or

- stone-filled vent trenches, often placed around the periphery of the landfill site.

Landfill leachate

Landfill leachate can pollute or contaminate both ground and surface water supplies. The degree of pollution will depend on local geology and hydrogeology, the nature of the waste (and, in turn, the leachate composition), and the proximity of susceptible receptors.

Groundwater flow rates can be very slow and are often measured in metres or tens of metres per year. Consequently, pollution may only be identified long after the event by which time remediation may impossible or too expensive.

While both the unsaturated (vadose) and saturated (groundwater) zones can attenuate some pollutants, **prevention** is the key to protecting the environment.

In the context of this report:

Pollution means 'the introduction by man into the environment of substances or energy liable to cause hazards to human health, harm to living resources and ecological systems, damage to structures or amenity, or interference with legitimate uses of the environment'.

Contamination means the introduction by man into the environment of potentially dangerous substances which do not *necessarily* constitute a hazard. Where a hazard is present the term 'pollution' is used.

Leachate production

Leachate comprises of the soluble components of waste and its degradation products which enter water as it percolates through the landfill. The amount of leachate generated depends on:

- Water availability.

- Landfill surface conditions.

- Refuse state.

- Conditions in the surrounding strata.

Box 21. The water balance equation

This equation, simplified below, is used in landfill design. Good practice normally requires that Lo is negative or zero so that no excess leachate is produced.

$$Lo = 1 - E - aW$$

i.e. $I - E < aW$

Where

Lo	=	Free Leachate retained at site (equivalent to leachate production minus leachate leaving the site)
I	=	Total liquid input
E	=	Evapotranspiration losses
a	=	Absorptive capacity of the waste
W	=	Weight of waste deposited

Water availability is affected by:

- Precipitation. This is the primary contributor to the water balance equation and cannot be controlled. It is essential to use rainfall figures at the design stage to ensure a net water deficit.

- Surface run-off, groundwater intrusion, irrigation. These can be controlled through effective site design and operation.

- Waste decomposition. This can be encouraged by providing optimal conditions.

- Liquid waste disposal.

Surface conditions affecting leachate generation include vegetation, cover material (density, permeability, moisture content etc.), surface topography and local meteorological conditions. Each of these factors can be measured (with varying degrees of accuracy) and inserted into the water balance equation to account for the total liquid entering and leaving the landfill.

Leachate composition and properties

Leachate composition varies with time and from site to site, and domestic waste normally produces the highest BOD leachate even if it is low in hazardous components. It is therefore difficult to describe a standard composition but the data in Table 10 are considered to represent typical acetogenic and methanogenic (See pH — below) leachates.

Leachate is hazardous due to its high BOD and COD content and the toxicity of dissolved organic and inorganic chemicals. If allowed to enter watercourses, aerobic metabolism of the high BOD/COD compounds can remove the majority of dissolved oxygen in the water, causing eutrophication and the death of fish and animal life.

Common toxic components in leachate are ammonia and heavy metals. The latter can be hazardous even at low levels if they accumulate through the food chain. The presence of ammoniacal nitrogen means that leachate often has to be treated off-site before it can be discharged to a sewer, since there is no natural bio-chemical path for its removal.

Leachate migration

In most cases it is impossible to predict accurately the movement of escaped leachate, but the main controlling factors are the surrounding geology and hydrogeology. Escape to surface waters may be relatively easy to control whereas escape to groundwater can be much more difficult both to control and to clean up.

The degree of groundwater contamination will be affected by physical, chemical and biological actions similar to those within the landfill. The relative importance of each process may change however, as the leachate moves from the landfill to the sub-surface region.

Table 10. Typical composition of Leachates from domestic wastes at various stages of decomposition (all figures in mg.l^{-1} except pH values)			
Determinand	Fresh wastes	Aged wastes	Wastes with high moisture
pH	6.2	7.5	8.0
COD	23800	1160	1500
BOD	11900	260	500
TOC	8000	465	450
Volatile acids (as C)	5688	5	12
NH$_3$-N	790	370	1000
NO$_3$-N	3	1	1.0
Ortho-P	0.73	1.4	1.0
Cl	1315	2080	1390
Na	9601	300	1900
Mg	252	185	186
K	780	590	570
Ca	1820	250	158
Mn	27	2.1	0.05
Fe	540	23	2.0
Cu	0.12	0.03	-
Zn	21.5	0.4	0.5
Pb	0.40	0.14	-

Notes on Table 10

pH
Methanogenic bacteria utilise available hydrogen, affecting bacterial growth in a way that favours production of acetate rather than higher acids. The net effect is to raise pH. So long as methanogenic activity continues, pH will remain near neutrality.

Chloride
The chloride ion is relatively unreactive and will undergo little or no retention as it moves through waste. It acts as an indicator of dilution, and can be used to map the leading edge of a pollution plume.

Organic Nitrogen
The decrease in organic nitrogen in methanogenic waste is a function of the microbial degradation of compounds such as protein. Protein appears to degrade rapidly during the acetogenic phase, producing high levels of ammonia. Ammoniacal nitrogen and organic nitrogen are differentiated.

Ammoniacal Nitrogen
Ammoniacal nitrogen is often present at high levels even in methanogenic waste. Once released within a landfill, there is no significant biochemical exit pathway for ammonia (Robinson and Gronow, 1992), making it necessary to treat leachate off-site before discharge to sewer.

TOC, COD, BOD
These parameters are measurements of carbonaceous content. Each reduces significantly in methanogenic waste due largely to the conversion of organic acids to methane and carbon dioxide. These acids represent the bulk of the organic carbon in leachate during the early stages of waste degradation (Pohland, 1975). More than 22% of the initial carbon content of MSW is exported as gas within 10 years of waste deposition (Belevi and Baccini, 1989).

BOD/COD ratio
This is an indication of the ration of biologically degradable carbon to 'total' (chemically oxidisable) carbon. It will reduce in methanogenic waste as degradable carbon decreases due to microbial activity.

Leachate control

The best way to control leachate pollution is through prevention, which should be integral to site design. In most cases it is necessary to control liquid ingress, collection and treatment, all of which can be done using a landfill liner.

Landfill liners (or covers) should be impermeable, durable, and resistant to chemical attack and puncture. They can be made from:

- Natural materials such as compacted clay or shale, bitumen, or soil sealants (bentonite); or

- Synthetic membranes i.e. geomembranes or flexible membrane liners (FML's).

Highly engineered liner systems will probably be too expensive for low income countries, but it is worth exploring the options as simplified variations may be viable in some situations (such as appropriate use of natural liners).

Natural liners (also called mineral liners) have the following advantages:

- Low permeability (though much higher than that of geomembranes).

- Relatively good resistance to chemical attack and punctures.

- Good sorption properties, enabling them to attenuate leachate as it migrates through the barrier.

Natural liners will not, however, act as true containment barriers; they are permeable, allowing leachate to migrate through them.

Synthetic membranes (geomembranes) are typically made of high density polyethylene (HDPE), or medium density polyethylene (MDPE). Their advantages include:

- Low permeability to most materials.

- Ease of installation.

- Relative strength and good deformation characteristics.

However, they also have disadvantages including:

- Slight permeability to some solvents.

- Risk of punctures or tears, especially during construction (construction quality is crucial).

- Very little attenuation capacity.

- Difficulty in forming impermeable seams between sheets, especially in unfavourable weather conditions.

- Expansion or shrinkage according to temperature and age.

Mineral and geomembrane liners are often used in combination to enhance the overall effectiveness of a containment system.

Where landfill gas and leachate are detected in existing landfills, remedial measures may be needed to reduce environmental risks. These may include

- Construction of vent trenches for landfill gas control, and

- Drilling of wells within the waste for the control of both gas and leachate.

Both systems work by creating a path of least resistance so the gas vents to atmosphere rather than migrating towards more sensitive targets. Where vent trenches are used, cost often restricts their depth to 5 metres; wells can be used for greater depths though this is expensive due to the difficult and heterogenous nature of the waste.

Leachate treatment
Clearly, the prevention of leachate migration cannot be guaranteed, and once it has happened, control and remediation is rarely possible. For this reason, and because we cannot remove or control the receptor (humans, plants etc.), leachate control at source is essential. This can be achieved via removal, treatment or both.

Leachate recirculation
One of the simplest forms of treatment is recirculation. A landfill acts as an anaerobic biological reactor, so recirculation of leachate enables further degradation and physico-chemical treatment of undegraded leachate components. This reduces the hazardous nature of the leachate, and helps to wet the waste, increasing its potential for biological degradation.

If recirculation is achieved by spray irrigation, leachate volume may also reduce through evaporation though this can cause atmospheric pollution by volatile organic compounds. It can also cause an unsightly crust of precipitated metal salts which create management problems. For this reason a leachate distribution system below the cap is usually preferable, though it is more difficult to engineer due to settlement and problems with pipework maintenance.

Chemical treatment

Chemical treatment of leachate is not common and where it was done in the past this was often for special purposes such as odour removal. More recently, hydrogen peroxide has been used as an additive to leachate before discharge to foul sewer in order to reduce problems associated with methane gas as it moves out of solution, and the associated explosion risks.

Generally, chemical treatment is not an essential component of appropriate landfilling in developing countries.

Biological treatment

Aerobic

Biological treatment to remove BOD, ammonia and suspended solids (with or without recirculation) is also common and aerobic processes tend to predominate. Aerated lagoons and activated sludge processes are often used for BOD and ammonia removal, while under conditions of low COD, rotating biological contactors (RBC's) can be very effective in removing ammonia.

Chemical treatment, activated carbon and reverse osmosis can be used for the removal of recalcitrant organics and trace hazardous organics not treated by biological processes.

Anaerobic leachate treatment has lower energy costs than aerobic processes and the amount of biomass produced is low. However, aerobic processes are often easier to control and operate, making them the preferred choice despite relatively high electricity costs. Landfill is in any case an anaerobic biological reactor, so little additional benefit is achieved by the use of further anaerobic treatment.

Summary

Landfill sites can present significant environmental and human health risks, however, by adopting a risk assessment approach, appropriate and cost-effective solutions may be identified. Controlling risks through effective waste management can be more appropriate than instituting expensive engineering controls and may also be more sustainable. For example, waste composting after segregation can reduce landfill risks and provide valuable material at the same time. Certain waste categories need special controls, for example, healthcare wastes. In most circumstances some landfill engineering control will be required and will be dependent upon a range of factors including:

- Waste type.

- Surrounding environment (site location).

- Climatic conditions.

- Availability of engineering materials.

- Availability of plant.

Landfill gas and leachate can present high environmental and human health risks, but control mechanisms are well known. Good site management can significantly reduce landfill-related problems.

References

Ali, S.M. (1998), *Source Separation in Karachi, Pakistan.* Paper prepared for WASTE, Netherlands (forthcoming).

Ball, J.M. (1998), *Regional Overview on Sub-saharan Africa.* In: Waste Disposal Workshop '98: Upgrading options for lower- and middle-income countries, Belo Horizonte, minais Gerais, Brazil, 8-11 September, pp.13-17, SKAT, Vadian strasse 42, CH-9000 St. Gallen, Switzerland.

Ball, J.M., Bredenhann, L. and Blight, G.E. (1993), *Minimum requirements for landfills in South Africa,* Proceedings Fourth International Landfill Symposium, Cagliari, Italy (Sardinia '93) vol. II, pp.1931-1940.

Ball, J.M., Bredenhann, L. and Blight, G.E. (1995), *Applications of minimum requirements for landfill design in Southern Africa,* Sardinia 95, Proceedings Fifth International Landfill Symposium, Cagliari, Italy (eds. Christensen, T.H., Cossu, R. and Stegmann, R.), pp.111-121.

Ball, J.M. and Langmore, K.L. (1996), *Update on the minimum requirements for waste disposal by landfill,* Proceedings, Wastecon '96, International Congress, Durban, South Africa, pp.78-88.

Ball, J.M. and Legg, P.A. (1997), *Views on appropriate landfill technology for developing countries,* Sardinia 97, Proceedings Sixth International Landfill Symposium, Cagliari, Italy, Vol. V (eds. Christensen, T.H., Cossu, R. and Stegmann, R.), pp.355-362.

Belevi, H. and Baccini, P. (1989), *Long term assessment of leachates from municipal solid waste landfills,* Sardinia 89. Proceedings Second International Landfill Symposium, Cagliari, Italy, Vol 1. CIPA, Milan, XXXIV, 1-8.

Bhide A.D. and Sundaresan, B.B. (1984), *Street Cleansing and Waste Storage and Collection in India,* Managing Solid Waste in Developing Countries, Holmes J.R. (ed.).

Blake, D.R. and Rowland, F.S. (1988), *World-wide increase in tropospheric methane, 1978-1988*, J. Atmos. Chem. 4, 43-62.

Buswell, A.M. and Hatfield, W.D. (1939), *Anaerobic fermentations*, Illinois State Water Survey Bulletin, 32, 1-193.

Coad, A. (1995), *Personal Communication*, Dr Adrian Coad, Lecturer, Loughborough University, UK.

Department of the Environment (1993), *Waste Management Paper 26A: Landfill Completion*, HMSO, UK.

EAUD (1991), *Pakistan National Report to UNCED, 1992*, Environment and Urban Affairs Division, Government of Pakistan.

ETSU (1992), *Review of the technologies for monitoring the microbiology of landfill*, Contractor Report ETSU B 1316, Harwell Laboratory, Oxon, UK.

Gendebien, A., Pauwels, M., Constant, M., Ledrut-Damanet, M.-J., Nyns, E.-J., Willumsen, H.-C., Butson, J., Fabry, R. and Ferrero, G.-L. (1992), *Landfill gas from environment to energy*, CEC, Luxembourg, ISBN 92-826-3672-0.

Harris, R.C., Knox, K. and Walker, N. (1993), *A strategy for the development of sustainable landfill design*, IWM Proceedings, Jan, 26-29.

Intergovernmental Panel of Climate Change (IPCC) (1992), *Climate change 1992,* The supplementary report to the Intergovernmental Panel on Climate Change Scientific Assessment, (Houghton, J.T., Callander, B.A. and Varney, S.K. eds.) Cambridge, UK, Cambridge University Press.

ISWA (International Solid Wastes Association) (1992), *1000 Terms in Solid Waste Management*, (Skitt, J. ed.). ISWA, Copenhagen.

REFERENCES

Javaid K. (1997), *Personal Communication*, Director Solid Waste Management, Karachi Metropolitan Corporation (KMC), Karachi, Pakistan.

Klundert A. (1996), *Final Report on Solid Waste Management in Karachi*, Karachi Metropolitan Corporation (KMC), Karachi.

Loxham, M. (1993), *The design of landfill sites — some issues from a European perspective*, Landfill tomorrow — Bioreactors or storage. Proceedings of seminar held at Imperial College of Science, Technology and medicine, London, pp.7-12.

Mohsin S. I. and Zubair A. (1994), *Chemical and Microbial Characterization of Groundwater of Karachi*, Poster papers of the International Conference, Helsinki, Finland 13-16 June, 1994, Publications of the Academy of Finland.

NESPAK (1992), *Detailed Design and Preparation of Tender Documents for Solid Waste Management*, Interim Report, National Engineering Services Pakistan (pvt.) Limited, Karachi, Pakistan.

ODA (1994), *Case Study of the use of Urban Waste by near — urban farmers of Kano, Nigeria*, Natural Resources Institute.

Petts, J.I. (1993), *Risk assessment, risk management and containment landfill*, 1993 Harwell Waste Management Symposium: Options for Landfill Containment, AEA Technology, Harwell, Oxfordshire, UK.

Pohland, F.G. (1975), *Sanitary landfill stabilisation with leachate recycle and residual treatment*, EPA grant R-801397, Georgia Institute of Technology, Atlanta, USA.

Robinson, H. and Gronow, J. (1992), *Groundwater protection in the UK: Assessment of the landfill leachate source term*, J.Inst.Wat.Env.Man. 6(2), pp.229-236.

Rushbrook, P.E. and Finnecy, E.E. (1988), *Planning for future waste management operations in developing countries,* Waste Management and Research 6, pp.1-21.

Rushbrook, P. and Pugh, M. (1998), *Solid waste landfills in middle- and lower-income countries: A technical guide to planning, design and operation*, SDC, SKAT, World Bank and WHO.

Schubeler, P., Wehrle, K. and Christen, J. (1996), *Conceptual framework for municipal solid waste management in low-income countries*, UMP working Paper Series No. 9 SKAT, Vadian strasse 42, CH-9000 St. Gallen, Switzerland.

Thurgood, M. (not dated), *Decision-makers' guide to solid waste landfills: Summary*, SDC, SKAT, World Bank and WHO.

UNEP (1996), *International Source Book on Environmentally Sound Technologies for Municipal Solid Waste Management*, IETC Technical Publication Issue 6.

Westlake, K (1997), *Sustainable landfill — possibility or pipedream?* Waste Management and Research, 15, 453-461.

Westlake, K (1995), *Sustainable landfill — the way forward*, Landfill Waste Pollution and Control, Albion Publishing Ltd.

World Health Organisation (1995), *Landfill*, Environmental Health Planning Pamphlet series No. 9, WHO regional office for Europe, Copenhagen, Denmark.

Bibliography

Blight, G.E. (1996), *Standards for landfills in developing countries*, Waste Management and Research, 14, pp.399-408.

Campbell, D.J.V. and Frost, R.C. (1997), *Landfill management, administration and regulations in developing countries.* In: Sardinia 97, Proceedings Sixth International Landfill Symposium, Cagliari, Italy, Vol. V (eds. Christensen, T.H., Cossu, R. and Stegmann, R.), pp.363-372.

Cointreau-Levine, S. (1994), *Private sector participation in municipal solid waste services in developing countries*, Volume 1: The formal sector, Urban Management Programme Discussion Paper 13, UNDP/ UNHCS/World Bank Urban Management Programme, World Bank, Washington DC, ISBN 0-8213-2825-5.

Diaz L. F. et. al (1996), *Solid Waste Management for Economically Developing Countries*, International Solid Waste Association (ISWA), Denmark.

IETC (1996), *International Source Book on Environmentally Sound Technologies for Municipal Solid Waste Management*, Technical Publication Series No. 6. UNEP, Nagoya, Japan.

MacFarlane, C.J. and Rushbrook, P. (1996), *Municipal solid waste management in middle- and lower-income countries*, WHO regional office for Europe, Copenhagen, Denmark, EUR/HFA target 23.

Rushbrook, P. (1997), *Encouraging better landfilling in middle and lower income countries.* In: Sardinia 97, Proceedings Sixth International Landfill Symposium, Cagliari, Italy, Vol. V (eds. Christensen, T.H., Cossu, R. and Stegmann, R.), pp.345-354.

Savage, G.M., Diaz, L.F., Golueke, C.G., Thorneloe, S. and Ham, R.K. (1997), *Landfill guidance document for developing countries.* In: Sardinia 97, Proceedings Sixth International Landfill Symposium, Cagliari, Italy, Vol. V (eds. Christensen, T.H., Cossu, R. and Stegmann, R.), pp.341-344.

Tchobanoglous G. et. al (1993), *Integrated Solid Waste Management*, Engineering Principles and Management Issues, McGraw Hill International Editions, McGraw Hill, New York.